INTEGRITY IN

HEALTH CARE

INSTITUTIONS

Integrity in

Health Care

Institutions

HUMANE ENVIRONMENTS FOR

TEACHING, INQUIRY, AND HEALING

EDITED BY RUTH ELLEN BULGER

AND STANLEY JOEL REISER

University of Iowa Press Ψ Iowa City

University of Iowa Press, Iowa City 52242

Copyright © 1990 by the University of Iowa

All rights reserved

Printed in the United States of America

First edition, 1990

Printed on acid-free paper

Library of Congress Cataloging-in-Publication Data

Integrity in health care institutions: humane environments for teaching, inquiry, and healing/edited by Ruth Ellen Bulger and Stanley Joel Reiser.—1st ed.

    p.   cm.

  ISBN 0-87745-300-4 (cloth: alk. paper)

  1. Hospitals, University—Moral and ethical aspects. 2. Medical ethics. I. Bulger, Ruth Ellen. II. Reiser, Stanley Joel.

  [DNLM: 1. Ethics, Medical. 2. Social Values.]

RA975.U5158 1990

174'.2—dc20

DNLM/DLC

for Library of Congress   90-11189

CONTENTS

PREFACE

The apparent collapse of the integrity of individuals has become a major concern in contemporary American society. Examples of individuals in government, business, education, science, and other professions who fail to live up to their avowed ethical standards are featured daily in our mass media alongside examples of those who are seen to maintain their integrity heroically. Yet most people spend the majority of their waking hours not just as individuals but within larger institutions—at work, schools, and religious or social organizations. We have been so absorbed for the past twenty years in considering the ethical relationships among individuals that the interaction between institutions and individuals has gone relatively unnoticed.

As a society, we are beginning to appreciate how an institution's values can have far-reaching effects on those within and outside its walls. Thus it seems appropriate that those who govern institutions and set policies for them should become aware of the ethical implications and effects of explicitly or unconsciously chosen values. In like manner, those employed within such institutions should be aware of how the institutional values have an impact on their own moral positions, altering them in positive or negative ways.

All sectors of our society have been affected by the loss of public trust resulting from a perceived diminution in individual and institutional integrity. Nowhere, however, is this diminution of trust more potentially devastating than in our health care and higher educational institutions, which intersect in our nation's academic health science centers. This book focuses on these issues as they relate to our university-based health educational and care programs, where caring and truth-seeking connect in a unique setting.

We begin by looking at the relationship between values expressed by institutions and those of individuals. We then consider the university and its roles in forming and transmitting the traditional educational values of expanding and conveying knowledge. Finally, as institutions assume an ever greater role in health care services, education, and research, it is important to understand how the values underlying institutional actions and policies are selected and what influence these values have on the treatment of both patients and those who serve as staff within the walls of the institutions.

We hope that the careful planning that went into the ordering and selection of essays and essayists will be evident to the reader, and that the complementary kneading and shaping of the material which emerged from the interchanges among the essayists during a conference held on the subject in Houston in June 1989 have integrated their ideas more fully. We deeply appreciate the efforts of the Josiah Macy, Jr., Foundation, the University of Texas Health Science Center at Houston, and the Association of Academic Health Centers, whose collective institutional support made this work of individuals possible. Finally, we hope that reading this collection of essays will entice you to join us in the effort to analyze these issues.

Introduction

ROGER J. BULGER

COVENANT, LEADERSHIP, AND

VALUE FORMATION IN

ACADEMIC HEALTH CENTERS

We are embarking upon an ambitious effort in seeking to explore what is implied by the title *Integrity in Health Care Institutions*, because the word *integrity*, in addition to denoting honesty and honorableness, means adherence to a code of values. There is an assumption then that institutions—academic health centers in particular—operate from a set of values; values which are either explicit in the institution's rhetoric or implicit in its behavior; values which are not necessarily consistent with each other or with some overarching conception of the center. We must admit, too, that there are some for whom the question is open as to whether or not an institution can or should or must have an overarching value system or purpose which transcends its own survival; this book, however, has been organized on the premise that even if an institution is seeking only its own survival, it is in fact expressing values which have an impact upon the individuals associated with it. Therefore, we seek to explore how an institution defines and expresses its values, how those expressions affect people both inside and outside, and ultimately, if we can, what an ideal set of such values might be for a modern academic health center, against which its institutional integrity can be measured.

In these introductory comments, one might expect a reflection upon a hierarchy of values beginning with the human and descending through societal, then professional, and finally personal values. Alternatively, one might simply reflect upon the value questions associated with the various major activities of the academic health center, such as teaching, patient care, and science. Or one could begin with the societal roots of the institution and dissect its array of accountabilities based upon those roots. There are other ways to approach these issues in an orderly, rational analysis, but I shall leave that effort to those who follow, who are more expert than I in these arenas.

My role is to introduce the issues related to institutional values, individual values, and the necessary interplay between them in the life of any complex organization and to indicate how massively important such matters can be. Assuming that institutions do operate from a value base to which, at their best, they should remain true (the definition of integrity), I will examine the interplay among the nature of these values, the institutional leadership which must sustain, support, or put these values into operation, the commitment to those values of the people who make up the institution, and the external forces which have an impact upon the institution. I shall make this introductory attempt through sometimes slightly idealized examples from my own experiences as the CEO of two academic health centers and from the perspective of a twenty-five-year career in academic medical and health administration in five different institutions in five different regions of the country. I will use specific illustrations in order to establish that there are important issues needing further analysis and significant problems needing attention of the sort that will be provided in the essays which follow.

If it is reasonable to conceive of institutions as having values, then we may ask, in our pluralistic society, who sets those values for the institution, how widely shared are those values across the institution, and, finally, how consistently does the institution express these values? The academic health center seems at times lately to be caught between the traditional values of the university and those of teaching hospitals striving to remain alive. All too often these tensions are recognized but apparently not understood for what they are by the people experiencing them. The same thing could be said about conflicts between the operating value system of the university and the expectations of the public or of society. How often, we may ask, are institutional values spelled out, debated, modified, and finally accepted by a critical mass of the institution's people or their outside sponsors? How often, on the other hand, is it assumed that the institution's values are what a concerned individual—whether dean, student, faculty member, president, or departmental chair—assumes them to be? I'm afraid that the latter is the rule rather than the exception.

One fundamental obstacle to institutional integrity built around a societal and university ideal is the serious tendency to isolate the health science centers from the rest of the university. The reasons for this trend are complex, but there is no doubt that there exists a drive for separateness on the part of academic health center people which is complemented by a tendency on the part of university officials to isolate the health care monsters on a kind of physical or administrative game preserve. How wide does our sense of community extend? Does an oral surgeon, plastic surgeon, or otolaryngologist belong more in the department and the national specialty group than in the school, the health science center, the university, and the community at large? The answer is probably yes! Admittedly, the key question is: can these specialists subordinate the interests of the former groupings to those that relate to the larger constituencies and communities? Still one wonders whether it is too much to hope that someday, for most people, the school, the health science center, the university, and society at large can achieve a more important place than the specialty group on the list.

Recognizing that those who follow are better suited to analyze the hierarchy of values that may ultimately lead to a mission statement for an academic health center, I should like to begin with the declaration of a mission statement in order to trace the interplay among the various players as implementation is attempted.

I have always considered higher educational institutions to be moral agents, agencies having covenantal relationships with the society which nurtures them. This view is perhaps best stated by William F. May in *The Physician's Covenant*:

> Institutions, consciously or unconsciously, embody a covenant, a social purpose, a human good, which they avow and serve, and in the course of rendering that service, institutions receive as well as give to the community. At one time, hospitals, largely charitable (in the sense of philanthropic institutions), perceived themselves as givers alone (though the poor often had to consent to experimentation to receive care). Under a third-party pay-

ment system, the buying and selling of the marketplace has largely replaced the philanthropic ideal of giving. The managers of a modern hospital think in terms of massive selling of services and behind its token philanthropies lies a covenantal base of giving and receiving that ought to infuse it. The community, after all, charters its life, grants it protection, and endows its enterprises with a public significance to which it must respond.[1]

Steven Schroeder and his colleagues in a recent paper marshall the available evidence to support the view that the academic health sciences are public trusts and that until academic health science centers realize this and act as though it were true, the public will be less and less inclined to support them.[2] Building upon these ideas of May and Schroeder et al., I propose that our hypothetical academic health center should have a mission statement that begins as follows: "The mission of the academic health center is to improve the health of the people . . ." The statement would then be rapidly expanded by adding words like these: ". . . by educating competent health professionals, by creating new knowledge, both basic and applied, by establishing model practice arrangements, replicable elsewhere, by delivering care of the highest standards to a significant number of people, and by educating patients and the public on matters of health promotion and disease prevention." In addition, I would add a second element as follows: "For the future, to continue to provide a basis for hope for further advances."

If we assume that such a mission statement by some legitimate process becomes the mission statement for the institution, we must next ask whether the statement is accepted by enough of the institution's major players to be effective, or whether there are some "shadow" missions which have more of a hold on the institution's energies. Is the stated mission the functional mission? Does the mission statement accurately reflect the institution's vision and does the vision reflect the key values common to a critical mass of people within the organization?

In order to move on to another level, let us assume that the institution has developed a rhetoric which promotes the values of competence, compassion, and commitment built upon a foundation of honesty and integrity. Further, let us assume that our hypothetical institution has recognized that institutional behavior is a pedagogical tool, serving as a kind of corporate role model, for better or for worse, for its faculty and students; since pedagogy is the institution's business, institutional behavior is crucial to the teaching and learning environment.

Now the stage is set for a discussion of leadership and the kinds of conflicts that often emerge from attempts at implementing this sort of plan.

If the role of the leadership is to move the institution forward according to a plan tied to a code of some sort, then a series of goals is likely to emerge from an aggressive strategic planning effort. As particular goals are determined and strategies and budgets are developed to achieve those goals, resistance naturally emerges and becomes increasingly more intense from those for whom this institutional mission and its derivative goals were never truly compelling. Thus the first type of conflict that is encountered can be referred to as a conflict of paradigms. For example, the reductionist biomedical model begins with organ physiology and gross anatomy and moves progressively to the molecular level, seeking to identify disease in precise molecular terms and to find equally precise molecular therapies. However, the currently emergent and dominating societal problems of violence, suicide, substance abuse, homelessness, and the prevention of AIDS are problems of populations, demography, and epidemiology—areas not likely to seem academically relevant to traditional medical faculty. Confusion and conflict are certain to develop should such traditional, biomedically oriented faculty perceive an inappropriately large proportion of scarce resources being directed away from molecular studies to what they regard as ultimately less productive activities.

A second type of conflict emerging from efforts to have an institution live up to a code of behavior may be called the insider/outsider conflict. If one takes the usual view implicit in most strategic plans, objectives are usually directed toward externally recognized targets or groups. Thus, if we start with improving the health of the people as the institutional mission, it would not be unusual that the institution's own people might be overlooked in the plan. To demonstrate a commitment to improving health, the institution should be led to develop internal programs aimed at improving employee, student, and faculty life; examples of such activities might be smoking and substance abuse prevention and cessation programs, enhanced safety and risk management programs, exercise and weight reduction opportunities, and promotion of exposure in the workplace to the liberal, performing, and visual arts. If institutional behavior is a pedagogical tool, then policies toward employees and students should reflect the values which are to be promoted among learners. Therein lie the seeds of some interesting conflicts between an administration perhaps too eager to bring everything into a neat alignment with an overarching philosophy and important people within the institution who don't share all aspects of that philosophy, especially when employees and students are involved.

A third kind of conflict in implementation arises out of the ambiguous interface between academe and business, between the academic function and the corporate function of the university. All too often, faculty feel the administration ought to get faculty input before implementing something, while the administration might see no reason to change its ways to coincide with behavioral characteristics recommended by the faculty for pedagogical purposes or simply to reflect an academic ethos.

Initiatives addressing a host of issues flow in sufficient profusion from this model of an overarching philosophy linked to strategic planning to keep any administration and institution busy, if not overwhelmed, especially if prudent choices and priorities aren't established. Among these many potential academic health center initiatives based on the improvement of the health of the people are items such as equal treatment for all, including women and racial minorities; integration of the various professions into a health care team; technology transfer for commercial benefit; establishment of model group practices, including interprofessional comprehensive delivery efforts; development of significant health promotional activities including community-associated efforts at reducing violence, elder- and child- and wife-abuse, drug and alcohol abuse, and so forth; programs in aging, health law, ethics, and health policy studies; programs for faculty development in teaching and in science and service programs generally not often enthusiastically supported, such as many in the mental health area, forensic psychiatry, problems of third world nations, and perhaps most importantly the restructuring of clinical education around the ambulatory setting.

Having made a hypothetical list of possible targets for concerted activity on the part of the academic health center, let us explore what resistance can be developed and obstacles raised to their accomplishment, with an eye toward the nature and art of leadership.

It should be noted at this point in the narrative about our hypothetical academic health center that the highly research-oriented institution can justify itself as best working to improve the health of the public by accomplishing first-rate research, just as the community-based institution emphasizing health service delivery and doing little cutting-edge research can justify its emphasis as the best way to support the public health interest. Let us assume that our model institution is a more representative academic health science center than either of the two extremes just mentioned and seeks to make balanced efforts in research, education, patient care, and community service. Let us now examine five different, sometimes competing, views of institutional integrity and ethics, each of which will find strong followings among important constituencies within the institution. These five views (or accounts as I shall refer to them) are not the only competing views bearing upon how an institution defines the functioning code to which it shall aspire. Nor are the five accounts mutually exclusive; they must, however, be addressed and dealt with on an ongoing basis if a critical mass of the internal and external constituencies is to support a consistent set of institutional values. These five accounts are as follows: the public interest or social utility account, the human values and social justice account, the traditional university account, the biomedical or molecular biology account, and the existential, inertial account which proclaims that what we are now is good enough, and which is exemplified best by entrenched individuals who are relatively happy with the way things currently are.

The public interest or social utility account assumes that the academic health center cannot fulfill its public trust without directly addressing the major health problems of the day. In a 1989 interview, Lee Cluff, the president of the Robert Wood Johnson Foundation and a distinguished professor of internal medicine, observed that he has never been able to understand how so many of the world's greatest academic medical complexes could develop and continue to prosper in the midst of some of society's most urgent problems and continue to fail to address those problems as a community service. Clearly he thinks academic health centers can and should do more.

Steven Schroeder and his colleagues have recently developed the thesis that academic health centers, both public and private, are public trusts, although they are not behaving that way often enough or intensely enough to meet rising public expectations. They warn that not to reverse this pattern is to risk a loss of public trust such that financial support for the institutions may become compromised.

Responsible adherents to this account advocate institutional involvement in all appropriate ways in efforts to visibly address society's most pressing health problems, while not compromising education and research missions. Critics of this approach see it as an effort to turn everything into a short-term answer to a social problem, while endangering the achievement of the time-honored goals of the modern health university. The poor will always be with us, they say; it is not the university's fault that they are there, nor is it the university's role in society to remedy their circumstances.

Former Senator Thomas Eagleton recently developed an interesting slant on academic health center leadership in the public interest:

> Never more than now have we needed leadership to develop a rational, equitable, cost-conscious health policy that recognizes and addresses the needs of our fast maturing population.
>
> Never more than now have we needed the health care community in its broadest sense to step forward with imaginative, creative, and thoughtful experiments in reorienting our national health policy.
>
> Never more than now must the medical community voluntarily enter into the formulation of policy rather than letting itself be dragged along as a reluctant but necessary partner as it was in the 1960s.[3]

Eagleton's answer to critics of the social utility account would be, for example, to admit that the academic health centers can't solve all the health problems of the poor, but they can certainly get into the policy process which bears upon how society will deal with its public problems.

The human values and social justice account has proponents who tend to relate institutional actions to their impact upon human beings. For example, Albert Jonson, in discussing the ethical dimensions of leadership in a 1987 address at a meeting of the Association of American Medical Colleges, targeted first the lack of humanity so often exemplified in patient care settings in the typical teaching hospital:

> I do not accuse the academic medical center of unethical prac-
> tice but only of being the place where the carefully refined tenets,
> learned in academic medical ethics, about decisions to forego
> life-support, informed consent and refusal of treatment, confiden-
> tiality and so on are almost systematically extinguished. The ac-
> ademic medical center is like the tavern that stands around the
> corner from the church: a sermon on temperance, however elo-
> quent, can hardly overpower the impulse to drop in and have a
> drink.
> There is a gap between what is taught about medical ethics
> and what goes in the clerkship and residency programs . . .

Jonson then likened medicine to religion, noting:

> Religion calls humans to the love of the divine; but churches
> and synagogues own property and collect tithes. Medicine is dedi-
> cated to healing the ill, but medical centers must meet the pay-
> ments on the construction loan, negotiate with the house officers'
> union, raise faculty salaries, and buy lithotripters and magnetic
> resonance imagers . . .
> . . . Yet like religious institutions, the noble purpose seems
> overwhelmed by the worldly concerns. Justice seems hardly a
> problem when survival is at stake . . . Ethical leadership de-
> mands courage and creativity, the willingness to tip the bal-
> ance toward the noble purpose, rather than to guard closely the
> worldly interests . . .

Finally, Jonson reflected further on leadership:

> Ethical leadership is, of course, particularly perilous . . . aca-
> demic health centers that fail to meet the problems of justice in
> health care will survive, but they will lose the luster of the an-
> cient and the new ethic of medicine—the ancient ethic which
> required absolute fidelity to the suffering patient and the new
> ethic which calls for a just and fair provision of service to all in
> need. Ethical leadership is nothing more than a brave willingness
> to take risks in favor of these values and an intelligent ingenuity
> in finding ways to realize them.[4]

According to this account, the academic health center should first see to its ethical output in terms of its dealing with people. Compassion, competence, commitment, and caring should extend from the way the institution treats its faculty and staff, to how the students are treated by everyone, to how patients, clients, and the public are treated by the institution. From staff development to faculty advancement to management of student and alumni affairs, issues of mercy, justice, fairness, and human development should take precedence over many other values. The diagnosis and treatment of such things as racism and sexism would be high on the institutional agenda, as would attempts to deliver care to those otherwise unable to get it or unable to pay for it. One can readily see how in the eyes of critics of this account, the ideal role model for a prudent manager can become transformed by those favoring this account into a Mother Teresa or a Saint Francis. Alternatively, one can also see how some elements of the university would worry about how easy it might be for such an ideologue of a leader to become another Ayatollah Khomeni.

The traditional university account would place primary emphasis on the transmission and generation of knowledge and would make all other values secondary to that basic mission. Thus, for example, rigorous safety standards in research laboratories and fire and safety codes of various sorts may be seen as unseemly intrusions into academic life—bureaucratic inventions designed to confound the research efforts of the faculty (as well they sometimes may be!). The current national exposure to allegations of fraud in science has brought some of these legitimate faculty concerns to the surface in the form of resistance to bureaucratic processes established at the national and university levels to insure accountability and to some basic procedural steps to safeguard the integrity of government-sponsored research. The argument goes as follows: the potential for loss of academic freedom far outweighs the possible gain by reduction of fraud in science supposed to result from these bureaucratic initiatives. These important values and important voices may have been too long overshadowed in the academic health center by the dominance of the financial ups and downs of teaching hospitals and clinical practice plans.

The biomedical or molecular biological account represents the thrust that has brought American health care to its preeminent position in the world over the past fifty years. Its advocates appropriately argue that their paradigm, which seeks answers at the molecular level, is still quintessentially fruitful, and some would argue that it deserves all our effort and attention. Don Seldin, in his most articulate statement of this position, argued that problems not fitting this paradigm should be taken care of by nurses and social workers.[5] The whole patient and the ambiguities of mental health are not mainstream in this modern mainstream medicine paradigm and will not be until and unless they can be dealt with in precise molecular terms.

This paradigm is not, therefore, broad enough to include all the legitimate interests and activities of an academic health center, but its proponents are often the major contributors to the center and they deserve to be cherished. They, on the other hand, tend not to suffer fools gladly and don't take readily to expenditure of resources for activities they perceive as being ultimately fruitless. Still, many of modern medicine's most prominent spokespersons, like Paul Beeson, David Rogers, and Al Tarlov, are strong advocates of an expanded medical model more along the lines of George Engle's bio-psycho-social medical model.

The existential or inertial account is that one which, despite rhetoric and evidence to the contrary, bestows upon its advocates an almost absolute and implacable commitment to preserve the environment, the turf, the institutional priorities, and the allocation of resources more or less as they are. This band of hardy souls tends certainly to provide stability and constancy of purpose to any institution; their numbers are swelled periodically by the ranks of those who favor change but don't favor the changes under consideration at that particular moment by the institutional leadership. Thus, they form shifting consortia of institutional bits and pieces which become important obstacles in virtually any significant alteration (whether good or bad) in institutional objectives and goals.

If one revisits now some of the examples of goals and objectives our hypothetical academic health center established for itself and considers each from the perspective of the five different acounts of the purposes of the institution, it is readily apparent that every goal and objective listed would be variably supported and resisted by different factions in the institution. If one considers the role of leadership in such an institution, one can equally readily see how tension and conflict will follow the person who seeks to implement efforts toward achieving these new goals. Such a circumstance should not be surprising. Institutional leadership from departmental chairs on up is invariably selected by broad-gauged search committees whose membership reflects a wide array of concerns. Such committees usually select people for their capacity and potential to effect change and to be imaginative and creative in utilizing the requisite management tools to allow the institution to react flexibly to the changes in the external environment. Once the selection is made, however, the search committee is disbanded and the new leader is measured as often as not by people marching to a different drummer than that of the original search committee.

In many of our institutions, that drummer is tranquility and peace; thus the leader who causes noise in the system may well become annoying and ultimately expendable. People resisting change from within the institution frequently are expert at creating just that noise in the system which is most annoying to trustees and regents and politicians. Therefore, the potential for achieving substantive change may be frustrated by an overly aggressive approach by a leader who then all too often becomes the target of those seeking a personnel change at the top, or it may be frustrated by the avoidance of the turmoil any prudent leader might anticipate after assessing the costs and benefits of moving forward on various issues. Thus we find institutions where for several years at a time, all the forces are in synchrony and extraordinary gains are accomplished; or there is relative tranquility and little progress; or there is relative turbulence with frequent leadership turnover and less than optimal progress to show for it.

The job of leadership, for example, in a Japanese corporation is a different matter from leadership of an American academic health center. In the former, the manager can count on the fact that everyone supports the corporate priorities which are, in descending order, employees, customers, suppliers, and then stockholders. No such analogous concurrence on value priorities exists in many American academic health centers and that makes leadership difficult. Thus, I am left to wonder whether our definition of leader and leadership needs to broaden. A manager of tranquility may from time to time be constructive and creative at a given institution, but as a steady diet, such cannot pass for leadership. On the other hand, a manager running around from one quixotic windmill charge to another is hardly the answer. A leader might be asked to carry out and to help lead the implementation of goals determined broadly within and without the institution involving all the important constituencies. A leader will need to continue to educate and remind those constituencies of what their agreed-upon goals are, but the faculty, students, and administration should not passively await the exposition of institutional values by the chief executive officer. This is perhaps the appeal of the bottom-up strategic planning model, wherein everyone theoretically participates in determining mission, goals, and objectives.

Leadership, then, in terms of moving an institution, is in my view largely dependent upon, if not identical with, a process—an ongoing process by which institutional values, goals, and directions are determined and made explicit with the broad involvement of faculty, staff, and students operating within guidelines established by the governing body of the institution. People in prominent positions within the institution can then be expected to move forward toward those goals, whatever their favorite particular account may be; this assumes of course that the sense of community which binds all the parts to the overall institution is sufficiently strong to overcome the centrifugal forces of perceived professional, specialty, intellectual, or personal self-interest. The intersection of institutional values and individual values often occurs precisely in the offices of the department chairs, deans, managers, and the chief executive of the center. If these leaders are to be expected to lead in the direction of fulfilling an institutional code or covenant, then they need to be supported in those efforts by people above and below them in the administrative chain, even if such a path leads to a periodic lessening of the "noiselessness" too often placed highest on the list of administrative virtues. An appropriate kind of institutional support involves an appreciation of the multiple external constraints acting upon most CEOs and a willingness to participate in honest communication loops among administrators, faculty, staff, and the student body.

In at least partial answer to the question of whether there ought to be explicit values targeted as parameters against which one could measure institutional integrity for academic health centers, and against which we could measure our leaders as more than managers, I offer two current items for consideration.

1. At a recent meeting comparing American and Canadian health care, an administrator of a large Canadian hospital who had spent

many years in the U.S. as a hospital administrator observed that his Canadian colleagues at the workaday level talk about improving patient care while his American colleagues seem only to discuss maximizing income, minimizing expense, and increasing market share. To the extent that this observation of a gross misappropriation of values is true, it seems to me to cry out for the attention of our academic health centers.

2.   Of the thirteen stories covered on the front page of the April 14, 1989, edition of the *New York Times*, nine dealt with dishonesty, cheating, and ethical failures in government, sports, business, investment banking, and science; three dealt with killings and bombings; and one dealt with broken promises in a failed experiment in the city of Rochester where teachers were used in a broader role than is traditional, but a role to which they had committed themselves in exchange for a dramatic increase in salary one year before.

It seems self-evident to me that, at every level, we Americans are seeking greater integrity from each other and from our institutions; we want our institutions of higher education—and our human service institutions especially—to remain committed to the highest ideals; and we want institutional leaders who can help bring these things to pass. It has been my purpose to indicate some of the forces which tend to inhibit a full expression of institutional integrity, setting the stage for my colleagues who can now clarify the muddied waters I have stirred and the conceptual ambiguities I may have created.

By using the device of describing a hypothetical academic health center with an overarching philosophy and well-articulated code, I have tried to illustrate how far-reaching (and therefore creative or dangerous or anxiety-producing) such an approach can become. It should be equally apparent that too rapid a forced movement can cause great strains within any institution, providing an argument perhaps for not getting too involved with explicit institutional philosophies, opting instead to muddle through on the basis of implied and assumed values.

It is often said that personal integrity is the responsibility of the individual. If that is kept intact (and no one can violate another's own integrity), then one is fundamentally on target as a person. Without that integrity, in spite of all other virtues and qualities, the individual will be fundamentally off target. Although the codes which must guide institutions are much more difficult to develop, and their covenants with society less widely appreciated, cannot the same generalizations about integrity be made for institutions as for individuals?

NOTES

1. William F. May, *The Physician's Covenant* (Philadelphia: Westminster Press, 1983), pp. 175–176.
2. Steven A. Schroeder, Jane S. Jones, and Jonathon A. Showstack, "Academic Medicine as a Public Trust," *Journal of the American Medical Association* 262 (August 1989): 803–812.
3. Thomas F. Eagleton, "In the Eye of a Hurricane," *Journal of Medical Education* 62 (February 1987): 83–85.
4. Albert R. Jonson, "Leadership in Meeting Ethical Challenges," *Journal of Medical Education* 62 (February 1987): 95–99.
5. D. W. Seldin, "The Boundaries of Medicine," *Transactions of the Association of American Physicians* 94 (1981): lxxv–lxxxvi.

The Role of Institutions

STEPHEN TOULMIN

MEDICAL INSTITUTIONS AND

THEIR MORAL CONSTRAINTS

Since the end of World War II, the focus of medical attention and
the locus of medical care in the United States have shifted away
from the individual doctor's office to hospital clinics and medical centers which are larger, more complex, more impersonal, and highly capi-
talized—not to mention bureaucratic. This change has also given rise
to social and ethical problems that we are in a position to understand
only now, in the late 1980s, and it will be a matter of great delicacy—
both moral and political—to resolve them.

The reasons for these changes are in part technical: the outcome of
admirable and hopeful advances in the armamentarium of clinical
care. The improvements in the treatment of infectious diseases resulting
from the development of antibiotic drugs, before and during the years of
war from 1939 to 1945, reduced the need for delicate and prolonged
clinical monitoring and so cut down the need for routine office and
home care. Scarlet fever, for instance, changed from a disease requiring
weeks of careful management to a strep throat with a rash, which sulfa
drugs quickly clear up. Meanwhile, new ways of diagnosing and treat-
ing graver conditions have increasingly involved technological devices
and machines that are within the financial reach only of the largest
and richest medical institutions. From being places of last resort, devoted to emergency or terminal care, hospitals have become places
where life support may be prolonged for months or even years. In both
respects, it is hard not to feel thankful for the new powers which we
have now achieved.

At the same time, there is a darker side to the picture. The current
shift from doctor's office to large-scale medical center has other, social

causes: in this respect, the profession of medicine is following along a path already traveled by many other institutions in modern society. The growing institutionalization of social life in the nineteenth and twentieth centuries has long been a matter for general analysis and comment, whether in the military or the church, in education or social services. By the 1920s and 30s, when medicine was still mainly a field for individual entrepreneurs, historians and sociologists had already been recording and analyzing the bureaucratic modes of operation in other sectors of society for a long time. Some of them, indeed, had come to the conclusion that increasing differentiation of social functions is a leading feature of the growth of modern society, and that the resulting tendency toward bureaucracy and institutionalization is an unavoidable long-term trend in the development of all advanced industrial nations.

This idea was canvased in the mid-nineteenth century by the English sociologist Herbert Spencer, and it was carried further around the turn of the century by Emile Durkheim in France and Max Weber in Germany. Both Spencer and Durkheim were influenced by analogies between social history and organic evolution: these led them to see increasing rigidity and complexity of structure as a price to be paid in the course of social evolution for progressive functional differentiation. The more narrowly we define and specify the social roles or job descriptions of the agents in our institutions, they concluded, the less room there will be for the exercise of flexibility and discretion in the performance of those roles. This whole process was even canonized by satire in Robert Musil's masterpiece, *The Man without Qualities*. "How difficult it is to be an individual these days," Musil's hero reflects. It is as though all social roles have gone on the stage so that, in the world of the twentieth century, the best we can do is to find pre-scripted parts into which we can cast ourselves, like actors joining a play all of whose lines preexist.

This essay will concentrate on the implications of this sociological perspective for contemporary medicine. The technical reasons for the new emphasis on large-scale institutions of medical care and research are by now a commonplace, but we do not yet fully appreciate either the social reasons for this change or the constraints that they place on the exercise of moral autonomy and discretion by physicians working within such institutions. The existence of these constraints is widely remarked on and complained about, but the fact that such problems are endemic to large-scale institutions of all kinds is not sufficiently noticed or taken into account. In this respect, the question of integrity in institutions raises issues that go far beyond the special features of medicine, and we may benefit from looking at them, for once, in the light of more general historical and sociological considerations.

We have tended to look at medical institutions too much in isolation and have failed to see how far large hospitals are just complex institutions *comme les autres*. Certainly, the tendency to centralize the delivery of health care in such large institutions presents great and challenging opportunities to medical research and practice: in this respect, highly organized medical institutions have the same merits as highly organized institutions of other kinds. But they have the same defects, also, and, for anyone seriously concerned with medical ethics, some of those disadvantages are extreme. The central concern of the present essay will be, in particular, the constraints that the process of institutionalization places on the scope for *moral* practice in medicine, and it will attempt to suggest what kinds of steps are needed if we are to counteract the worst of these side effects on medical ethics.

The darkest view of this topic is that of the German sociologist Max Weber, who died in 1920. In a series of fine works on the theory of social and economic organization before and during the First World War, Weber painted a picture of modern society as headed inescapably toward greater differentiation of social roles and increased bureaucratization in the operation of institutions. His famous and telling image represents society as approximating more and more the condition of an "iron cage." In a fully differentiated and bureaucratized society, everybody's duties and responsibilities will be defined precisely in advance. As a result, professional callings will be displaced by job descriptions; ethical obligations will give way to functional imperatives; personal shame and individual responsibility will be replaced by institutional excuses and evasions. When the claims of professional integrity and institutional survival come into conflict, victory will inevitably go to the stronger. In any head-on conflict, institutions are more powerful than individuals, and this will lead to the progressive devaluation of the moral claims of professionalism in the interest of insuring the economic fortunes and proper functioning of the institutions concerned. What Aldous Huxley, the novelist, imagined in *Brave New World*, Weber had already predicted as a soon-to-be-realized fact of social history.

For anyone interested in Max Weber's analysis, the present state of American medicine in general and the modern hospital or medical center in particular is a rich source of illustrations. Whether we consider the matter from the standpoint of a hospital administrator, a practicing physician, an individual patient, or the patient's relatives and lawyer, current developments can be viewed as realizing Weber's prophecies almost to the letter. These developments are described as follows.

1. Hospital administrators feel obliged by outside authority and economic pressure to establish procedures aimed at defending their institutions' budgetary soundness and public reputation; and this is, of course, entirely proper. It is precisely their job to do so. If one incidental by-product of these administrative procedures is a refusal to accept some patients who lack insurance coverage ("dumping" patients), it no doubt strikes the individual administrator as a sad necessity about which he or she may feel a purely personal chagrin.

2. Meanwhile, the physicians who work in large hospitals and medical centers see these administrative procedures as limiting the scope for their exercise of professional discretion and forcing them to practice their Hippocratic profession in a selective rather than a generous-spirited way. This perception, too, is largely correct, but too often the physicians' sense of these limitations is so strong that they interpret the procedures in a conservative and cautious spirit, rather than risk endangering their position in the institution. This reaction is quite understandable—no one can blame the medical staff of a large hospital if they choose, by and large, to be team players rather than whistle blowers—but its effects are, to say the least, unhappy. Doctors who are worried about protecting their privileges or their staff positions are less able to focus their minds directly on the immediate needs of their patients.

3. As for the patients who receive their medical care within such institutions, they cannot be blamed for measuring the realities of personal interaction within a present-day hospital clinic against the romantic image, which the profession still likes to project, of the doctor-patient relationship at its closest and warmest best. As a result, patients often enough become suspicious of the physicians with whom they have to deal, and read their institutional caution as a

lapse from the moral commitments which patients have been taught to expect.

4. As a result, the mishaps and other bad outcomes that, in some proportion of cases, inevitably follow medical treatment in a hospital or medical center unjustly come to appear as evidence of carelessness, negligence, or even downright incompetence and so cry out for legal remedy. This perception is, of course, grist to the mill of a personal injury lawyer whose business is, quite properly, to place the burden of proof on a hospital or physician to show that a patient's treatment was proper, the injury not reasonably foreseeable, even unavoidable, and so not an occasion for a malpractice verdict or for damages.

The technical advantages of practicing medicine within a large institution are, thus, purchased at the price of substantial social and ethical *dis*advantages. Whether or not these perceptions of the present situation are or are not entirely correct is not the point: either way, the delivery of medical care within large hospitals does tend to be shaped by these perceptions. To the extent that this is so—to the extent that, in the operation of a modern hospital, the claims of budgetary survival tend to outweigh those of a moral calling—the institution verges on the condition of a tyrant. To that extent, too, medical practitioners collectively cease to be a profession, and the individual doctor's work, circumscribed by institutional imperatives, is removed from the sphere of moral commitment and placed within the realm of social necessity. To that extent, in short, the physician's work is *de-moral-ized.*

This verdict may sound harsh, even exaggerated; but it captures a tendency of which all perceptive physicians today are quite well aware. Recently, I read the fine discussion of the *Antigone* in Martha Nussbaum's book, *The Fragility of Goodness,* as well as the play itself, with a group of physicians at the University of Chicago. Discussing the tragic conflict when Creon, the tyrant of Thebes, forbids Antigone to perform the death rites for her brother, whom Creon sees as a traitor, the physicians in our group—without prompting—fell into a discussion of what they called the "Creonization" of the modern hospital.

At this point, many people are unhappy to leave the reality of the pressures and constraints unexamined and return to these questions: how far is this perception of the imperatives that govern the operations of hospitals and medical centers *no more than* a matter of perception? How far does it represent pressures and constraints that are real obstacles to the moral practice of medicine? Surely—they suggest—to the extent that the perception is inaccurate, there is nothing to worry about, since we have an effective remedy at hand. All that is needed is for the different agents in this situation to recognize the falsity of their initial perceptions and to understand that they are free to act with greater moral courage and initiative.

At this point, however, the sociological perspective begins to have a real bite. *The social effect of institutionalization and bureaucratization is the same, whether people's perceptions of that effect are accurate or inaccurate.* In Durkheim's phrase, the "social facts" responsible for the actual operations of institutions *are* the perceived constraints to which the agents who work within them see themselves as being subject. In this respect, perceived constraints function as real constraints. Whether or not a hospital's financial condition makes patient dumping indispensable, the pressure to give priority to patients with insurance coverage is inescapable. Whether or not hospital physicians need to worry about endangering their tenure, the risks inherent in doing an end run around the hospital's procedures are undeniable. Likewise, whether or not patients justifiably suspect that members of the medical staff are less fully dedicated than they hoped, their fear of such neglect will color their relations to those staff members, and so on.

To put the point in a nutshell: whether or not these perceptions are realistic or unrealistic, they operate in exactly the same way. We know that those who work in institutions are liable, in practice, to overstate the risks to which their position exposes them: "Better safe than sorry," they say. Quite understandably, the treasurers of hospitals are inclined to set overly rigid rules against admitting needy but uninsured patients. Quite understandably, physicians hesitate to end the use of life support systems even in some hopeless cases and rationalize their hesitation by referring to the supposed danger of the hospital being sued by the family. Quite understandably, patients overinterpret and resent the effects of paperwork and other seeming irrelevancies on their medical treatment. For equally understandable reasons, attorneys versed in tort law are a trifle too quick to see medical mishaps as implying actual incompetence. The most efficacious social facts in the actual hospital situation are, in real life, *those perceptions themselves*, not the objective risks and needs as these might be assessed by some impartial, outside observer. (As Dr. Engelhardt put it in discussion, "Hospitals are risk-aversive.")

It may be that our medical system could accommodate the needs of a few more uninsured patients without disaster. It may be that no court has ever, in fact, found against a physician in a damage suit arising out of conscientious termination of life support. It may be that, even though two dozen people on a hospital's staff have legitimate reasons to read a patient's chart, medical confidentiality in fact remains largely inviolate and protected. It may be that only a very few medical bad outcomes are fairly seen as evidence of actual negligence or incompetence. As long as institutions are structured so as to embody the imperatives about which Max Weber wrote, the perceived situation drives the agents involved as effectively as any actual needs or risks.

The fact that our social perceptions are inaccurate, or only partly accurate, is thus no help. In the social realm, as Durkheim and Weber both understood, perceived constraints are real constraints. The fact that they are inaccurate can even make them more, not less, powerful. (In journalism, notoriously, self-censorship by news media is even more restrictive and damaging than frank censorship by external authority.) Those of us who are involved in complex medical institutions cannot, therefore, plead innocence and escape criticism on the grounds of good intentions. Instead, we must come to terms with the undesired, but largely inescapable, side effects of the new institutional structure of medicine and, by reflecting on this analysis, come to see how those side effects might, at least in part, be counteracted. That is the other question to be faced in the present essay.

The answers to that question are neither simple to establish nor easy to agree upon. In order to reach a provisional diagnosis, it will be helpful to look at the history of some other enterprises which took the road of institutionalization earlier than medicine did. In this respect—to repeat—medicine is following in the footsteps of other enterprises within which much has already been learned and whose experience offers us a number of helpful insights. The central questions are as follows.

1. Is the organization of human activities in large institutions compatible with continued exercise of *any* professional discretion by the agents who work within such institutions?

2. Do the imperatives of institutional organization imply the suppression of professional discretion and moral responsiblity in favor of established procedures and policies, *in all cases alike*?

3. If, within such institutions, a measure of protection can be given to professional ethics *in certain cases*, on what conditions can such protection be provided, and what is special about the cases in which this can be done?

The different kinds of enterprises that are useful parallels to medicine fall on a spectrum: some of them have been more, some less successful in protecting the claims of moral obligation and professional discretion. Let us look, here, at a few samples.

Consider, to begin with, the institutions by which human services of nonmedical kinds were provided to those in need, at different stages in the social history of Western Europe and North America. Before the mid-eighteenth century, this was primarily the responsibility of ministers, priests, and other church officials. At that earlier stage, of course, what we now call welfare was known by the name of charity; but, like public education and the care of the mentally disturbed, it fell to religious organizations to help those in need, within the limits of the available resources. Regarded as institutions, the churches were in some respects as complex and highly organized as any institution in the modern world: notably, they had definite hierarchical structures and clear divisions of responsibility. In other respects, ministers and parish priests had a real measure of discretion in deciding which of the families or individuals under their wing were the most deserving, and in dividing up the resources available for charitable purposes in the light of those judgments. Once in a while, no doubt, a priest or minister was suspected of misusing this discretion and was thereby left open to reproof, or even discipline, by the bishop or the congregation, depending on the custom of the denomination. But this situation was exceptional. As a rule, it was presumed that any minister of religion could be trusted to make such decisions with an eye to the relative needs of the possible beneficiaries: equitably, rather than in conformity with a fixed book of rules.

In modern democratic states, by contrast, the need to insure that officials dispensing welfare do so accountably restricts to a minimum the scope for discretion and substitutes general, rule-governed equality for particular judgments of individual equity. In a modern state, welfare benefits are typically allocated, or withheld, in a rule-governed manner, designed to insure uniformity of treatment among all who satisfy the established set of criteria. Clerks in local social security offices have only minimal power to make any discretionary decisions. If the delivery of medical services is analogous to the delivery of human services of nonmedical kinds, then, the following question arises: can physicians in large-scale medical institutions be given the chance to work more like ministers of the church and less like social security clerks? The problem of protecting the professional standing of medicine within the new institutional context thus requires us to maximize the range of decisions over which individual hospital physicians can be encouraged to exercise professional discretion.

The analogy between health and welfare is not the only one to tell us something useful about the problems of institutionalized medicine. Moving to quite another point on the spectrum of human enterprises, let us consider the way in which, with industrialization, the production of material goods shifted from individuals to factories. During the last forty years, members of the general public have increasingly come to conceive of modern medicine, not in terms of the individual physician's judgment and experience, but as a collective resource which is in theory available to benefit all patients alike. Rightly or wrongly, the institutional network of modern medicine is, for them, a unity with powers, knowledge, and skills as much superior to the powers, knowledge, and skills of the patient as the powers, knowledge, and skills of General Motors (say) are superior to those of the average car buyer. From this point of view, individual physicians appear less like priests, more like sales reps: their responsibility is to deliver the best medical goods the collectivity of medicine has yet devised. This being so, physicians can no longer afford to operate by the seat of their pants, like William Carlos Williams' "Old Doc Rivers": instead, they are generally expected (not least, by the courts) to keep up to date about the latest research and the most advanced treatments relevant to the patient's condition.

In other enterprises, for example, the auto industry, the corresponding shift had important legal consequences. For a start, American law imposes on car manufacturers (and other producers with "deep pockets") a stricter form of liability for injury than it does on normal individuals, who have no special position of superior power, wealth, or knowledge. In the auto industry, for instance, the doctrine of strict liability goes back to the case of *McPherson v. Buick*. There, a woman was injured when the brake cables in her new car failed, and she was awarded damages against the car manufacturers, on the basis that they could more easily insure the safety of their products than the purchaser could prove that they were negligent in failing to do so. Proof of negligence was waived, and the fact of injury by itself was made the occasion for redress.

The more the delivery of health services is institutionalized, the more the general public shows signs of wishing to impose on doctors and hospitals a similarly strict liability for the bad outcomes of medical treatment. Increasingly, that is, medical injury is viewed as entitling the victim to redress, aside from any need to establish actual negligence or incompetence. In industry, the imposition of strict liability arose out of a recognition of the imbalance of power between makers of complex consumer products, such as cars, and their eventual purchasers. Just as the average medical patient cannot assess the acts of clinical judgment that go into the treatment he or she receives, so the average car buyer cannot monitor the quality of the materials and procedures that go into the product that he or she buys. So, juries are now liable to find for plaintiffs against hospitals on the patent evidence of injury, without insisting on conclusive evidence about who did what wrong, and how.

In material production, then, the shift from the work of individuals to the elaborate organization of the modern factory has led to a new set of relations between manufacturers and purchasers. Not all the effects of this change have been bad. On a strict liability standard from which the stigma of actual negligence has been removed, monetary damages are replaced by something more like compensation. Injuries in the workplace, for example, are typically made good by payments out of a workers' compensation fund. Such payments are more predictable, and also less onerous, than those assessed by juries by way of tort damages. They are more easily covered by insurance, and the business of running a compensation scheme is less risky and speculative than is present-day malpractice insurance. Such a compensation scheme already exists in New Zealand, where members of the general public can be compensated for injuries suffered as the result of a wide range of accidents, medical mishaps, and other misfortunes which are made the occasion, not for assessing damages, but for payments by way of compensation.

As matters stand, in malpractice cases, hospitals and public alike tend to talk as though the proper goal for medical treatment were one of zero errors. As a result, it is difficult for hospital physicians to admit publicly that their error rate is in fact nonzero or for hospital administrators to establish realistic procedures for monitoring error rates in the different clinics or departments of a hospital. Yet, arguably, the myth of zero errors is a dishonest pretense: it puts an unreasonable load on physicians and prevents the discovery of realistic base lines for evaluating the actual errors and mishaps that creep into the best-administered medical service.

Finally, experience in the field of appliance production has shown by now that it is not merely feasible to decentralize decision making in large organizations: in many cases it is more efficient. One example is the Volvo experiment: the Swedish car maker replaced its existing production line, in part, by work teams of a dozen or so workers who were responsible for assembling complete cars while deciding among themselves how to split up the necessary work. Unlike the mechanical production line of the 1930s—and Taylor's time and motion studies, as caricatured in Chaplin's film *Modern Times*—the Volvo scheme led to an improved rate of production while giving much more discretion to the workers in the production teams involved.

If the medical profession is to face the opportunities and challenges that have been created by the centralization of health services in large institutions, they will have to ask whether the lesson of the Volvo experiment, for instance, has something to tell hospital administrators and physicians. Relieved of their misperceptions of the imperatives that operate in such institutions, hospital physicians may thus regain more elbow room for professional discretion, and protect the moral aspects of their practice that are at present under threat.

There remains serious doubt whether (as Dr. Pellegrino puts it in his essay) any collectivity—for example, a hospital corporation—can, as such, be a moral agent at all. However much we are tempted to think of the Menninger Clinic as a noble institution or as a morally admirable experiment, the nobility and admiration attach in fact to Dr. Menninger himself. The problems that face clinical medicine in an age of large institutions will in the last resort be solved only in part by restructuring their procedures. Beyond that, the leaders of the institutions must display moral courage if they are to insure that the medical professionals who are the heart and core of hospitals and clinics continue to practice their art according to the moral demands, and with the moral integrity, that physicians required of themselves (and one another) in earlier, more individualistic times.

The topic of integrity in medical institutions, in short, does not just refer to the problem of maintaining the integrity of those institutions: that is, avoiding bankruptcy and protecting the hospital's public image. That duty comes naturally to hospital administrators and helps to reinforce, not counteract, the social pressures we have looked at in this essay. Rather, the problem is to protect the moral and professional integrity of medical practice, when that practice takes place within an institutional setting: that is, to find ways in which the moral thrust of medicine need not be blocked and the professional standards of the physician can be maintained, in the face of all the imperatives on which the institutional survival of the hospital may seem to depend.

This challenge is one that calls for strong, imaginative leadership from the top: above all, from the president of the institution, but also from its board of trustees and from the professional associations. It is a problem that has no easy solution and demands continual effort. (The price of integrity, like that of freedom, is eternal vigilance.) The chief executive of a hospital or medical center must, of course, listen to the financial staff and to the public authorities who have a stake in the hospital's work, but, in the end, must answer the treasurer and the government in the same way: by refusing to be driven by arguments of necessity into policies and actions that compromise the integrity of the hospital's physicians. Faced with calls to set further new procedures in place, for bureaucratic reasons, the chief executive must instead assemble an ethical impact statement, to determine whether the new procedures will not further limit the doctors' opportunity for honest, conscientious practice.

Not for nothing do we think of medicine as a calling, whose deepest motives are shaped by the physician's moral commitment. From now on, leadership of a high order is needed if, within large medical institutions, this standing is not to be compromised.

H. TRISTRAM ENGELHARDT, JR.

INTEGRITY, HUMANENESS,

AND INSTITUTIONS IN

SECULAR PLURALIST SOCIETIES

The crisis of the late twentieth century, and perhaps of the next millennium, is that just as we are on the threshold of acquiring immense biological capacities to cure disease and through genetic engineering to alter fundamentally our genome, we are most unclear about what goals should guide us and what moral constraints should limit our endeavors. Recent reflections about postmodern culture and ethics are in large measure symptoms of this fundamental intellectual breakdown. The difficulty of developing humane environments for teaching, inquiry, and healing is that intellectually we can no longer justify the optimism of the Renaissance and the Enlightenment regarding the capacity of reason to be a surrogate for God. We do not agree about the moral significance of *humanitas*, *humanus*, humane, or human nature. There are deeply conflicting views of the status of the fetus, the role of welfare, the licitness of euthanasia, the integrity of institutions, and the ultimate meaning of humane existence. We are faced with a plurality of moral understandings of the significance of humanity and of the human condition, just as we need most to create a common vision that will guide us in educating the healers of the twenty-first century. It is no longer clear what it is to be *an* authority on human values or who is *in* authority to resolve major moral and ethical controversies and to guide social institutions. We are confronted with deeply troubling questions. Can we speak of values without being either hopelessly vague or stridently divisive? Do we share enough of a moral vision when we meet as moral strangers, as individuals from different moral communities, to justify a general ethic for secular institutions? Or is moral life in the postmodern world too irresolvably fragmented?

THE POSTMODERN PREDICAMENT

How can we talk of humane institutional environments for health care unless we can establish whether we still share a common secular vision of humanism and humane action? This is both a philosophical and a historical-cultural question. We live this side of a number of profound cultural changes which have conspired to bring institutions and their authority into question. These changes have also brought into question our ability to frame a concrete secular moral vision. As I have already suggested, this difficulty can be captured by the designation "postmodern age."

The division between the ancient and medieval eras has been seen in terms of the establishment of Christianity as the regnant ideology and world view for the West. What Cassiodorus termed the modern era is what we have come to identify as the Middle Ages. The institutions of the Middle Ages presupposed not only that there are unique revealed truths which provide authority for action, but in addition that reason is able to establish general moral guidelines binding upon believers and nonbelievers alike. In short, the Middle Ages strengthened many of the Stoic and other views of natural law that were already developed in the ancient Roman world to provide fundamental constraints upon social institutions. It provided a much more robust understanding of *jus gentium*. As a result, during the Middle Ages there was an assumption that a generally justifiable answer could be given to questions regarding the integrity of institutions. There were disagreements. However, there was also the assumption that individuals share enough in common to know who is *in* authority to resolve disputes. Moreover, there was a sufficient common understanding of the moral enterprise so that most participants could in principle agree on what it means to be *a* moral authority, to be an expert regarding the proper conduct of educational and healing institutions.

In its official communality of vision, the Middle Ages contrasts sharply with the ancient world. The ancient world was a place of skepticism, divergent moral views, and competing moral visions. There was no single established, concrete religious or ideological viewpoint. Rather, a heterogeneity of understandings of moral institutions marked the period. One might indeed take the polytheism of the ancient world as a metaphor for the pluralism which flourished in it.

The Renaissance, with its revival of interest in ancient languages and learning, which gave renewed strength to interest in humane action and humanism, can be seen as a return to these antique sensibilities. There was an enthusiasm for Graeco-Roman culture, images, and literary devices. There was an attempt to recapture the vibrancy and strength of the pre-Christian world. But there was a difference. The modern world created by the Renaissance continued to embrace the monotheistic metaphor. Though many became nonbelievers, they sought through reason to establish a surrogate for the Christian God. That is, the framers of the modern world, from the Age of Reason through the Enlightenment and even into the twentieth century, presumed that men and women simply as humans share enough to establish a content-full, canonical moral viewpoint that can convey moral authority to the central institutions of society. There has been the assumption that one can meaningfully talk of a common, content-full moral framework, even after rejecting the authority and moral vision provided for social institutions for nearly a millennium by the Christian God.

The modern age emerged as a counterculture. It was framed against the long reign of Christianity. Still, because the modern era maintained the key medieval metaphor or image of a basic moral foundation or content-full moral vision that can be shared by all, it was closer than often appreciated to the Middle Ages. But, to borrow a metaphor from Nietzsche, the Modern Age did in fact finally kill God. Indeed, it did more than kill God in the sense of removing God from his previous central place in western culture as the foundation of institutional authority and moral vision. Modern culture also killed man. That is, modern culture has, in the end, removed human nature as a source of moral authority. Human nature is, after all, from a secular perspective, the result of blind evolutionary forces and natural happenstance. In short, not only is God dead, but following

Foucault's metaphor, man is dead as well.[1] We no longer share the common understanding of *humanitas* or of *humanus* that was the source of our traditions of humanism and natural law. As a result, it is questionable whether we share, or if we do share, whether we can justify a general moral, content-full understanding of the goals of social institutions. This profound moral and philosophical catastrophe should not be that unexpected.

For the last two millennia we have somewhat innocently exploited the fertile and seductive ambiguities of *humanitas*. Even classical authors such as Aulus Gellius (c. A.D. 130–170) noted that the term was already used in his period to identify both learning and philanthropy.[2] The various rich and interweaving meanings of humanism can be gathered under three rubrics, all of which have been put into question in the postmodern era. First, humanism has been associated with a set of canonical scriptures, or at least a literature, which is uniquely western, in particular Graeco-Roman. It was, after all, this literature which provided the impetus for the Renaissance, and which has been the recurring focus of pleas to revivify the humanities and to recapture the core of our culture.[3] However, in the postmodern world, western literature, in particular the classics, appears as merely one culture's product against many others. Second, humanism as a particular tradition of humanitarian feelings is just as arbitrary. Sympathy is always shaped, at least in part, in terms of particular views of the other's good. As a result, humanitarianism must in the end be understood in terms of the third sense of humanism: an appeal to a set of philosophical arguments regarding the normatively human, the ways in which humans should act with each other and fashion social institutions.

The difficulty is that, though humans may generally agree regarding important social desiderata, there is great disagreement about how to rank these goals. Even if one might grant that individuals generally wish through social institutions to secure prosperity, liberty, and equality, quite different institutional arrangements and views of integrity and humaneness will appear plausible, depending upon how these important moral goals are ranked. There is no non-controversial way to establish the correct ranking of fundamental social goals or the selection of a canonical moral vision. One cannot appeal to impartial observers, hypothetical contractors, or other variations of hypothetical decision makers, without begging the question. Either such decision makers will already be equipped with the appropriate moral sense, or it will have to be smuggled in. One cannot establish any particular moral sense without an appeal to a higher-level moral sense or an already presupposed thin theory of the good.

The same can be said with regard to appeals to preferences. One will need to know which preferences are allowable or which are to be favored over others (e.g., do present preferences count the same as, more than, or less than future, likely better informed preferences?). Nor can one appeal to nature or consequences unless one can evaluate what one finds. One can sum up consequences only if one knows how to weigh liberty consequences, equality consequences, prosperity consequences, and security consequences. And if one rejects foundationalism altogether, one is left with propaganda, prayer, force, or peaceable negotiation. One may bewail this description of the state of affairs. One may abhor it. But disliking it will not exorcize the demon.

In short, the modern project of providing a single canonical grounding for the moral life, for the authority of social institutions, and for talk about humane institutions or the integrity of institutions appears hopeless. When moral strangers meet, there does not appear to be enough that they share as humans, as rational persons, to determine how they should cooperate, what they should hold to be important, or what kind of social institutions they should fashion.

One can use the term postmodernity to identify the collapse of the assumption that one can discover unambiguously who is a moral authority to determine, in general, the proper answers to content-full concrete moral questions regarding the integrity or humaneness of social institutions, or who is in authority to resolve moral disputes. In the contemporary era one is confronted with a world marked by a plurality of moral visions for which the metaphor of polytheism is again heuristic. Pro-lifers face prochoice advocates, Yuppies face Shiite Moslems, Palestinians face Hassidic Jews. Particular communities appear able, on the basis of appeals to faith, tradition, or specially informed views of rationality, to determine their own concrete fabric of morality and the proper structure for their social institutions. We return then to the troubling questions: do we still share enough in common so that when moral strangers meet, they can participate in and use secular social institutions such as those we find for health care and health care education? Which moral principles should guide such institutions? By whose standards can one determine their integrity or humaneness?

The situation is, as Alasdair MacIntyre has aptly described it, one of living with the shreds and pieces of once vital moral traditions.[4] We live in a world in which individuals attempt to frame general moral viewpoints using arguments and moral practices that have been removed from the original moral frameworks within which the arguments were developed, sustained, and justified. As a result, at the general secular level, one is left with fragments of once vital moral perspectives. On the one hand, one finds social institutions and parts of general arguments no longer articulated within a coherently justified moral framework. On the other hand, one still finds robust religious and ideological communities which face each other without the benefit of an independent, general, concrete mediating moral perspective.

The question remains: how do we in a secular world justify a general moral perspective that can compass the divergent communities that come in contact within health care institutions? And, how does one in such circumstances understand the moral place or position of those educational and health care institutions which are embedded, not within a general secular perspective, but within particular, often mutually hostile, moral understandings of human well-being and of good health care?

CONFLICTING VIEWS OF INTEGRITY AND HUMANENESS

How are divergent views of the proper goals and organization of social institutions to be mediated, if it is in fact impossible to identify as canonical a particular ranking of social desiderata or a particular concrete moral vision of the good life without begging the question in the process? If one is not to seek cloture to such controversies by appealing directly or indirectly to force, including the force of majorities, one will need to find a general moral basis for resolving fundamental moral controversies. However, it no longer appears plausible to appeal to a common grace given by God, as was the case in the Middle Ages. Nor will an appeal to reason, the core to the modern approach, function decisively. As Alasdair MacIntyre has noted in a recent volume, there is no single, unambiguous sense of justice or rationality.[5] One must always determine to whose rationality, whose justice, whose sense of humaneness, whose sense of integrity one is appealing. The problem then is to find a position from which one can choose among conflicting views of justice, rationality, humaneness, and integrity.

If one cannot discover a generally defensible basis for resolving such controversies by an appeal to the grace of God, to a particular content-full understanding of moral reason, or to a particular cultural tradition, then one will need to appeal to the consent of those who are interested in resolving issues peaceably. If one cannot appeal to God, tradition, or reason to establish moral authority, one can appeal to the consent of those who participate in common endeavors.

Such a derivation of authority does not require a particular hierarchy of values, endorsing liberty as having a prior claim over other values, or seeing democracy as a particularly efficient way of organizing social institutions. Rather, institutions that draw their authority from common consent, not God or reason, are those which are most plausibly justifiable when moral strangers meet, individuals who do not share a concrete moral understanding of the good life or the proper character of social institutions. One does not need to share a concrete view of the good life or of humane institutions in order to negotiate peaceably, as the market shows. The justification of limited democracies, of rights to privacy, of free and informed consent, and of the salience of individualism is grounded more in a skepticism regarding the discoverability of a concrete, content-full view of social institutions than in any special value given to individuals or liberty.

The emergence of limited democracies in the nineteenth and twentieth centuries, along with an increasing emphasis upon rights to privacy and on the role of freedom and informed consent, can thus be regarded as more than a historical accident. These are ways of resolving moral controversies in the absence of the ability to discover correct answers. They are procedural structures through which individuals can convey authority and create answers.[6] This approach to the moral grounding of social institutions allows one to give a justification for their authority when moral strangers meet. It allows individuals who are members of disparate moral communities to collaborate even when they do not share a concrete view of the moral significance of human nature, the character of the moral life, or the integrity of social institutions. Procedural means of gaining moral authority can be abstracted from concrete moral values. In fact, a frequent characteristic of social institutions in secular pluralist societies is their procedural, contentless character. They seek authority from those who participate and emphasize tolerance and the right of individuals to exempt themselves from concrete moral understandings with which they disagree (e.g., rights to privacy).

Asking about the integrity and humaneness of secular institutions becomes somewhat like asking about the integrity and humaneness of the post office. It is not an impossible question devoid of a meaningful answer. However, when an answer is given, it will be articulated in terms of services provided to individuals, independent of their particular moral viewpoints, and with a sensitivity to those viewpoints insofar as that is required for providing the service.

One is thus confronted with the difficulty of framing secular institutions which may not in principle endorse particular concrete understandings of moral integrity or humaneness without ceasing to be neutral, secular institutions. The core understanding of integrity and humaneness in such institutions must be based on the project of peaceably acquiring the consent and authority of those who join in and support secular social understandings. Such institutions must at a minimum stress toleration and recognize the individual as the source of moral authority. Since individuals are generally interested in having their own views of the good taken seriously, secular institutions in pluralist societies will do best if they encourage the members of their institutions to understand the views of those who come for services and at least make clear the limits and capacities of those institutions. The humaneness of secular institutions will be defined in terms of general conditions for respecting persons. This will involve valuing toleration, truth telling, and attention to patients and clients. As a result, it remains important to understand the geography of human moral visions and the history of the development of views of integrity and humaneness. These traditional contributions of the humanities are central to enabling individuals in secular institutions to respond to the diversity of moral understandings and to anticipate the controversies that will need mediation.

Finally, over and against the constrained authority of secular institutions, private institutions emerge as the proper custodians of particular moral visions. They are what sustains the differences that make secular mediation important and interesting. If the moral visions of most assume the instrumental character parodied in some portrayals of Yuppies, there will be little of moral substance needing to be mediated by secular moral institutions.[7] But unlike those who are committed to instrumental goods and fair procedures, private institutions can pursue goals that are good in themselves and more dear than fairness. Secular institutions and private institutions can thus have strongly contrasting notions of integrity and humane conduct. The generality of secular institutions will unavoidably be purchased at the price of content. The integrity of a truly secular institution in a pluralist society is to be available to all, without excluding some because of a particular commitment to a particular set of values. Thus, secular institutions should ideally require only a commitment to the peaceable resolution of controversies and to the mutual respect required in order to garner moral authority.

Private institutions, in contrast, purchase content at the price of generality. To be a particular private institution committed to a particular set of values is to achieve a concrete understanding of integrity, of human nature, and of the purposes of human life. But such a concreteness will always divide "us" from "them," those who endorse the particular set of values from those who do not. Moral content and commitment are always divisive. However, they allow individuals to live within particular moral communities that have substantial moral traditions, which tell concrete moral stories, instruct individuals over generations, and sustain social institutions that can support rich visions of human excellence. The integrity of private educational institutions is to articulate their own concrete understanding of morality and humaneness, just as the secular institutions are to deport themselves in ways that make them accessible to all peaceable individuals.

INSTITUTIONS IN SECULAR PLURALIST SOCIETIES

In summary, when framing institutions in secular pluralist societies, one must attend to values at two levels if one wishes to support integrity and humaneness. First, one must allow moral communities with their integral understandings of human nature and of human values to survive in an increasingly secular world and to transmit their visions further. It is not simply that we all must live within a concrete vision, but that a forthright and vigorous discussion contrasting moral perspectives will be necessary, not only to guide technology, but especially to frame the institutions that will educate future physicians regarding what it is to take values seriously. The various moral viewpoints that contend for our attention must be recognized not simply as relics from the past to be maintained in the intellectual museums of historians of thought; they are, rather, key to our capacity to adapt to the technological challenges of the future while maintaining concrete moral visions. Only concrete visions really tell individuals why to use technology and when. But to talk across moral communities, we need a language for use among moral strangers, a second level of moral discourse. A secular society, which provides health care for individuals from numerous moral communities, will need, through its educational institutions, to help its health care students to appreciate what it is to mediate conflicting moral understandings in ways that respect the individuals who hold them, without denigrating the seriousness of the values they endorse. In this context, rights to privacy will take on a new salience and significance, and the values of tolerance and liberality will acquire new life.

NOTES

1. Claude Bonnefoy, "L'homme est-il mort? Un entretien avec Michel Foucault," *Arts* 38 (June 15, 1966): 8–9.
2. John C. Rolfe, trans., *The Attic Nights of Aulus Gellius*, XIII.xvii.1 (Cambridge, Mass.: Harvard University Press, 1978), vol. 2, p. 395.
3. I have in mind movements such as the Third Humanism and the New Humanism. See Horst Rudiger, *Wesen und Wandlung des Humanismus* (Hamburg: Hoffmann & Campe, 1937), and J. David Hoeveler, Jr., *The New Humanism* (Charlottesville: University Press of Virginia, 1977); see also Norman Foerster, ed., "Religion without Humanism," in *Humanism and America* (New York: Farrar & Rinehart, 1930), as well as Allan Bloom, *The Closing of the American Mind* (New York: Simon & Schuster, 1987).

4. Alasdair MacIntyre, *After Virtue* (Notre Dame: University of Notre Dame Press, 1981).

5. Alasdair MacIntyre, *Whose Injustice? Which Rationality?* (Notre Dame: University of Notre Dame Press, 1988).

6. For a study of this issue, see *Scientific Controversies: A Study in the Resolution and Closure of Disputes Concerning Science and Technology*, ed. H. T. Engelhardt, Jr., and A. L. Caplan (New York: Cambridge University Press, 1987). See in particular "Ethical Theory and the Product of Closure," by Tom L. Beauchamp, pp. 27–48.

7. For one portrayal of the ethos of Yuppies, see Marissa Piesman and Marilee Hartley, *The Yuppie Handbook* (New York: Long Shadow Books, 1984). One should note that the ethos of Yuppiedom is international. See, for example, *Das Yuppie Handbuch: Einblicke in die Lebens-und Konsumgewohnheiten der Young Urban Professionals*, trans. Volker Schmiddem (Berlin: Sympathie-Verlag, 1987).

ROBERT COLES

INSTITUTIONS AND THE

SHAPING OF CHARACTER

During the early 1960s, when my wife, Jane, and I lived in Georgia, we often went on Sundays to the Ebenezer Baptist Church in downtown Atlanta to hear the Reverend Doctor Martin Luther King, Jr., give his passionate and powerful sermons. It was also our privilege to know him. We were studying school desegregation under the auspices of the Southern Regional Council, and he was no stranger to that group of fine white and black people who were determined to change the racial situation in that part of the United States. Many times during those years I heard Dr. King talk about the nature of the institutions he was challenging so bravely and boldly: the schools, the universities, the offices of county sheriffs, the legislatures, the urban police departments, the restaurant and movie house chains, and not least, the federal government, its legislature, its executive branch, and its courts. I also had the distinct and unforgettable experience of spending personal time with Dr. King, listening to him as he reflected upon his struggles with those institutions, hearing him analyze their workings, take stock of their effect on the people of his native South, and contemplate their future in the better world he hoped to see emerge from all the turbulence which was then so much a part of daily life in Atlanta and other cities he knew and kept visiting.

One afternoon in 1964, I remember Dr. King saying this: "We are pushing hard on [southern] institutions because we want our people to change." I was surprised and intrigued. I stated the obvious: that people like him and those who followed his lead had already changed, and, indeed, were pressing those institutions to become altogether different in certain respects. Yes, he agreed, but he had his eyes on a larger vision: "We are a few; we are outsiders. In the long run it's the institutions that make people as they are. Who can avoid their heavy glare or their beckoning smile?" He stopped at that point, and for a few seconds the melancholy lyricism of his words held my complete attention. To be sure, I was soon enough reminding him that thousands and thousands of black people, no matter how terrible the weight upon them of decades of segregation, had nonetheless taken up arms willingly, eagerly, and at great risk, against all sorts of institutions. Hence they indicated an ability to be critical of institutions, to distance themselves decisively from them, even to take up moral and psychological arms against them, and so to change them, rather than be the unwilling or defenseless victims of their persuasive and commanding power. Again, he assented, but he wanted to nudge me further than I seemed willing to go: "Institutions are only a part of the story, I know. We learn to fight them (some of us!) as well as to bow to them. But they are a *big* part of the story. They do a lot to influence us." A pause, then this: "They can help us or they can hurt us; and they are important in our children's lives and in our lives. They help shape character."

That last phrase was put just right and has stayed in my mind ever since. More recently it has come up front in my thoughts as I have taught college students and medical students or worked with residents taking training in child psychiatry. Dr. King was telling a physician trained in psychoanalytic psychiatry that we become who we are not only by virtue of the psychology of our families but in response to the social, political, and cultural world around us—a world of money, power, and acceptance or a world of poverty, weakness, and rejection. He knew, of course, that children are strongly influenced emotionally and morally by their parents. But he wanted me to go further, to think of us as constantly being affected by the larger family in which we live as youths who have left home for school, as adults who live in cities, in regions, in a nation. After several years of involvement in the sit-in movement, I was quite prepared to go along with his way of seeing things. Yet I began to realize that this was not to his full satisfaction because he wanted to press upon me a degree of particularity and specificity that I found it convenient, perhaps, to shun. "You and I have values," he mentioned to me in that conversation, and then a tough follow-up: "So do companies and corporations and nations . . . and universities."

In one sense he had said the obvious, the uncontroversial. I remember thinking of the Bill of Rights as he spoke, the moral center of America's values, the bedrock of its character as a nation. I remember thinking, too, of the various values which companies uphold through advertising, or in the way they get along with their customers and their workers. But the values of universities hadn't really entered my mind. I had lived in them and studied in several, yet I hadn't thought of them, or the hospitals where I worked for years, as places where my own character had been or indeed was still being shaped. True, universities are places where knowledge is learned and imparted, and hospitals are places in which the sick are treated. Certain values are thereby being upheld: the worth of learning and of healing. For Dr. King, however, there was more to ponder, and soon enough, he had me doing so. For instance, I told him that when I was an intern at the University of Chicago in 1955, I rarely saw black patients, and when I did, they were kept away from the white patients—a tacit or informal segregation of sorts, even though the university hospital was literally adjacent to a growing black neighborhood on the south side of the city. I also told him, going back further in time, that my medical school class had only three women in it, only one black person, and my college class had only one or two blacks—all this in the *second* half of the twentieth century in the United States of America.

Such demographic information, of course, is also institutional information, and not least it is information that has a decided bearing on the moral and psychological life of those who keep making enormous commitments of time and energy to the institutions in question: students and teachers. "I live in this place, it's my whole life," a medical student told me in 1987, as we were discussing the courses he was taking and the words of advice he was receiving from various tutors, advisers, lecturers, and deans. I demurred a bit, mentioned other activities and involvements he surely had and their contribution to his mind and heart. He agreed, but he also held firmly to his overall point of view: "I don't have much time to spare. I only glance at the newspapers. I watch the evening news on TV, when I'm not out some place. I don't read the magazines—just *Time* at odd moments. I'm a medical student, that's who I am, and it's a full-time job. The people who run this place run me. They give us lectures, and we say yes. No, it's not just the memorizing I'm talking about. [I had asked.] It's their attitudes, their ideas; they look at the world in their own way, and they want us to have the same eyes they have.

"I went to see one of the deans the other day and asked him why this medical school pulled out of a hospital [one devoted to a city's poor, down and out people] and I got the run-around, lots of high and mighty excuses. I was almost ready to quote from the Bible—I had some of Jesus' words on the tip of my tongue—but I said to myself: this guy doesn't want to hear such talk. Keep pushing him with your Sunday school lessons and he'll call in a psychiatrist to give you the once-over: you having some problems, buddy? After a while you just give up; you start seeing things the way they want you to. They give you these highfalutin speeches, welcoming you at the start, and welcoming you back each year, and pretty soon you're talking to yourself the way they talk to you."

He was an idealistic young man who had been in the Peace Corps, who yearned for a medical education that connected him to the serious difficulties—physical and mental as well as social, racial, and economic—of the poor and so-called working-class people who lived not far from the classrooms he attended. When some of those people, for reasons they felt strongly, began picketing the administration building of the medical school he was proud to call his, he became increasingly troubled and, eventually, did see a psychiatrist to whom he was referred by a physician at the medical school's health services. Soon enough the two were grappling not only with the long-standing emotional troubles (who is without them?) but the more contemporary question of how one responds to a major political criticism of an institution which has become one's guide, one's sponsor, one's pathway to a future life.

"I sympathize with those people [picketing]," he told me one afternoon as we discussed the nature of his medical education and its ups and downs. He did not easily continue along that line. He paused. He made mention of his difficulties with a particular course. He went into a brief nostalgic reverie—a return to his two years in Latin America. He asked me about *my* views, my politics, my response to a neighborhood challenge directed at a rich, powerful medical institution. As I hesitated and qualified one assertion with another, he became noticeably ill at ease, then increasingly outspoken and voluble: "This place demands its dues. It does so in a quiet way—nothing pushy or vulgar here! The place absorbs you—it takes you in, and pretty soon 'the words of the boss are the words of the peasants.' I used to hear that expression from the peasants; they were smart as can be, in their own way, and they were telling me what they had to tell themselves all the time—the psychological power of power! You take your cues from the big shots who run things. What else can you do? Starve? Go without work? Become a loner who has to go from day to day—a job here and there, until the same old problem comes up: do you stand up for what you believe in, or do you learn to keep your mouth shut?

"Talking about keeping your mouth shut, one peasant said this to me: 'The longer you keep quiet, the harder it is to talk.' I think of him a lot these days. I think of him when I hear some dean or professor give us a talk—really a talking-to or a sermon—and I hear myself saying nothing, even though there's plenty on my mind to say, but I've turned off the motor. My shrink says I'm merely 'accommodating myself to the moment.' 'That's what you have to do,' he's said a hundred times since we began talking. Why? I want to know why. He shrugs his shoulders and gives me the same pieties I heard from those peasants, who never went to medical school or took residencies in psychiatry and training in psychoanalysis, and who never charged me a penny for their wisdom. 'That's the way it is,' he'll say, or 'life is compromising.' If I challenge those comments, he becomes stony in his silence, and I know I'm wasting my time and my limited supply of dough. There are days when I want to walk away and go back to Ecuador. There are days when—the worst days!—I don't notice those picketers, and I couldn't care less about them. They're a bother, a nuisance, a real pain! I hear the dean's voice, and I walk away fast and think of me, my life, my big deal future in medicine. You talk about Ivan Ilyich! I'm Ivan Ilyich, before his illness!"

He was making a reference, of course, to the Tolstoy story "The Death of Ivan Ilyich," which he had read in a course I teach. He was reminding me, really, that it is one thing to read a morally suggestive and compelling story and quite another to live one's life as one believes one ought to—the old and important and haunting distinction between a person's ideas and his or her conduct. So often, the institutional life we live is a crucial influence on us as we struggle with such a matter. Companies, corporations, universities—they all bear down on us, encouraging us in ways, discouraging us in other ways. Institutions give us sanction—a sense of worth that comes with being part of something larger, something tied to a given society's money and power, its authority. Institutions can also take their toll, demanding acquiescence or an all too significant degree of acquiescence. Hence my student's anguish. Hence my own anguish, too, on certain days, when I wonder why some people who work very hard in this world and do so much for others get little or no recognition from our universities, while others who are far less decent and kindly get constant honors; as I wonder if the day will come when White House state dinners and honorary degree ceremonies will feature not only generals, financiers, politicians, and authors, but also ordinary, hardworking people whose sweat and blood have built this country and all countries: the mother of one of my students, perhaps, a black woman who has run a Head Start center in Harlem for twenty years and has taken in dozens of abandoned foster children; or the father of one of my students, perhaps, a truck driver with no education who has worked day and night so that every one of his six children could finish high school and go to college, and even (three of them) go to graduate school.

In 1985, when Harvard celebrated its 350th anniversary by honoring some very important people, I thought surely a woman and man such as those two might have been up there with the best of them. It was an institution's way, at a moment filled with consequence, of declaring its values and helping to shape the values of those who are its teachers, its administrators, and its students. In the words of one of those students, already quoted above: "Sometimes the people who run this place [a medical school and the nearby hospitals] are ready to give you an out-and-out lecture on what's right and what's wrong, but a lot of days they say nothing to you about ethical issues. But what they're doing—the way they get on with the janitors, the cooks, the neighborhood nearby, the people they bow and scrape to, the people they won't give the time of day to—that's how we learn their values, and that's, maybe, how we get some of our own." With that comment he waited for a reply from me, but I could only register a silent nod as I remembered in my own life, yet again, the various moments not unlike the ones that medical student shared with me, in which one or another institution's decisions, policies, and pronouncements had given me pause. But soon, all too soon, they had brought my mind into tow—a dismaying testimony to a kind of psychology that goes all too unexamined in our universities in this twentieth-century secular world.

The University

DANIEL STEINER

APPROACHING ETHICAL QUESTIONS:

A UNIVERSITY PERSPECTIVE

Universities have traditionally occupied a very special place in our society. We entrust them with the education of our young and look to them to provide the trained people and leaders our nation needs. We expect universities to be the locus of important advances in knowledge that will benefit the environment, the economy, our health, and other important aspects of our lives. To be a faculty member at one of our many excellent universities is to occupy a respected position in our society. We are willing to provide, directly and indirectly, large amounts of public and private funds to support universities.

The special place accorded universities is based in part on the distinctive values they embody and the way they behave. As is evidenced by policy statements and speeches by presidents, universities profess to abide by values and to accept obligations different from those of other institutions. For at least two reasons it is timely to consider what these values and obligations are and to gain a better understanding of how to assess the policies and actions of universities in light of these values and obligations.

First, the special measure of respect enjoyed by universities seems to be eroding. Many observers of higher education see universities failing to act in accordance with their own values. Universities are perceived to be similar in important respects to other institutions in our society that act out of self-interest and without sufficient attention to principle. University lobbyists seek to shape the tax laws to favor higher education, and some universities hire specialized lobbyists to bypass the peer review process by gaining direct appropriations from Congress. Many major college athletic programs seem to be operated with scant regard for academic standards or the welfare of the athletes in order to serve financial and other interests of the institution. Racial incidents and incidents of attacks on unpopular speakers have been reported by the media with a disturbing frequency. Universities often appear to give insufficient attention to the misconduct of faculty members pursuing their research, and some faculty members seem to have inappropriately close ties to the world of commerce. In these and other ways, universities may be losing a measure of respect and their special place in our society.

Second, the ethical dimensions of university management have become increasingly diverse and complex. (By ethical dimensions I mean the rightness or wrongness of university policies and actions in light of the university's values and principles and its obligations to society.) A number of factors account for this development. The range of university activities has increased as universities have sought new ways to carry out their teaching and research functions and have expanded their relationships with other institutions here and abroad. Society has looked with greater expectations to universities to meet important needs, in education as well as in other areas. When examining actions and policies of universities, students and other internal constituencies have both questioned the commitment of universities to ethical standards and looked to universities for greater leadership on important moral questions of the day. The diminished respect for and increased mistrust of institutions in our culture have affected universities, whose actions have been examined with greater skepticism and held up to more demanding standards. New laws and the vexatious and frequently controversial questions presented by important social issues and problems of our time such as race relations, sexual harassment, disability, abortion, sexual orientation, and affirmative action have added to the mix. Shortages of money to carry out teaching and research have put pressure on fund-raising efforts and led to searches for other means of increasing income. In a multitude of ways these and other changes and developments in recent years have posed a variety of policy and practical questions with ethical aspects.

Facing ethical questions is essential, although it is understandable why they often do not receive the careful thought they deserve. They occur often and can be complex and divisive. In some situations they raise competing demands of apparently equal weight: they require time, attention, and sometimes much money to resolve. Moreover, the issues seem at times tangential to the core teaching and research mission of the institution; a harried faculty member, trustee, or administrator might well prefer to turn his or her attention to other problems. However, the damage can be enormous if universities fail to grapple honestly, directly, and openly with the perplexing ethical questions that arise on an almost daily basis.

A lack of attention to ethical questions can have several consequences. First, because unique values distinguish universities from other institutions, there will be a loss of sense of purpose and definition within the academic community. Such a loss is likely to be accompanied by a decline both in the quality of teaching and research and also in self-respect. Second, a university that pays too little attention to defining and articulating its values, understanding whether its policies and actions are consistent with its values, and explaining its conclusions is more likely to fail in its effort to teach its students to recognize and address ethical dilemmas in their personal and professional lives. Finally, inattention to ethical issues will lead to erosion of public support for universities, with significant tangible and intangible effects that will inevitably lessen the ability of universities to contribute to our knowledge and welfare.

When thinking about ethical questions, universities, like other institutions, can benefit from an articulation of the elements that are central to their consideration of such questions. Having such an understanding minimizes, among other things, the dangers of ad hoc analyses which are likely to result in a pattern of inconsistent decisions. For decisions on ethical matters to be understood and respected, even if not agreed with, it is important that they be based on consistent principles and modes of analysis.

Of necessity, each member of the university community will bring to bear his or her own personal values, perspectives, and approaches to ethical questions, but something more is needed when one is trying to answer a question or act on behalf of an institution such as a university. Different considerations bear on personal decisions and institutional decisions, and one's personal framework is not appropriate or sufficient when acting in an institutional capacity. Let me suggest, from the perspective of an administrator and lawyer at a private research and teaching university, some of the principal considerations that affect resolution of ethical questions by a university. I will do so by looking at the purposes or objectives of the university, the values that distinguish the university from other institutions and are necessary to achieve the objectives, and the responsibilities and obligations of the university.

The main objectives of a private teaching and research university can be stated in a variety of ways, all centering on a core theme: the preservation, discovery, and transmission of knowledge. The inherent premise is that knowledge per se is something of great value to our society, that knowledge can lead to improvements in our lives, and that institutions devoted to knowledge therefore serve an important function.

In the United States in the twentieth century two principles have emerged as essential to the university's ability to serve society most effectively as the setting for the discovery and transmission of knowledge: university autonomy and academic freedom. Taken together these two concepts help provide the unconstrained environment that is most conducive to creativity and learning.

University autonomy encompasses issues of governance that relate to the core of the academic enterprise. Universities must preserve the right to decide questions such as who will teach and do research, what will be taught, how it will be taught, and which students will be admitted. Society is willing to grant universities this autonomy for two reasons. One relates to the expertise of academics and a willingness to allow people with special knowledge and insight to make decisions that affect the pursuit of their disciplines. The second, I believe, is pragmatic and based on experience. The system works. Universities in the United States have achieved a very high level of excellence in an environment that encourages diversity and is relatively free of extramural control.

Academic freedom, although it has applications to questions of institutional governance, most often refers to the rights of individual faculty members. These rights, as they affect most directly the discovery and transmission of knowledge, concern the freedom to choose areas of research, to decide how to pursue the research, to publish freely the results of that research, and, when teaching, to present material in the classroom in ways of one's own choosing. Academic freedom also protects the extramural statements of faculty members.

If the concepts of university autonomy and academic freedom are to serve their purposes and if universities and academics are to continue to enjoy the protection of these concepts, there is a need to pay careful attention to issues of integrity and respect for individual dignity. Academic freedom quickly loses its purpose and meaning if the research or teaching processes become tainted by outside influences or by sloppy or dishonest practices. Society has a right to presume that academic freedom means that faculty members are ordering their activities and reaching conclusions in the laboratory or classroom in a manner dictated by their independent judgments and in accordance with professional standards. Similarly, institutional decisions and the institutional environment must recognize and protect the dignity of the individual and not clash with the core values of society that mandate respect for the individual. Institutional autonomy cannot, for example, be an excuse for racial or sexual bias or harassment. Nor can it justify suppression of speech, an action incompatible with the goals of the university and of society.

In the view of many observers of higher education, institutional autonomy also depends upon a degree of institutional forebearance—universities in their institutional capacity should not take positions on the wide range of social and political questions that concern the nation but do not directly affect higher education. There are two bases for this stricture. The first is a concern that institutional positions on social and political questions inhibit academic freedom. A perceived orthodoxy may have the effect of stifling opposing views.

The second reason stems from the belief that implicit in the compact with society that grants institutional autonomy is the understanding that universities will not be political actors. If universities want to remain free of outside control, they should not in their institutional capacities take positions on the full range of social and political issues of the day in order to influence governmental actions or use their economic power in an effort to get other institutions, such as business corporations, to behave in certain ways.

UNIVERSITIES AS CORPORATIONS

In its corporate capacity a university engages not only in teaching and research but in a variety of other activities that enable it to function. A university is likely to be a landlord, contractor, purchaser, employer, neighbor, and shareholder as well as a party to many other formal and informal relationships. Each of these relationships has its own set of values, obligations, and responsibilities to which a university must pay heed.

In this respect universities in theory are not markedly different from other corporations. The types of activities are similar and in many respects the ethical standards should be the same. But in fact there are important differences that stem primarily from a higher level of scrutiny and expectations. Both internal and external constituencies tend to watch universities more carefully than other corporations and expect them to conform to a more elevated standard of conduct. Universities are seen to serve a public purpose and may therefore be perceived as having a greater obligation to act in a manner consistent with the public interest as interpreted by different stakeholders within and outside the university community. Whether or not the higher standard is totally justified, it is a reality, and universities must recognize that the ethical component in their everyday dealings is something that requires careful and constant attention.

THE LAW

A third source of values, responsibilities, and obligations comes from the outside, from the legal system that governs the society in which the university exists. The law comes into play in a number of ways, and I will touch upon some of the principal ones.

There is, of course, the basic fiduciary responsibility of the trustees for the well-being of the institution, the preservation and growth of its assets, and the use of funds in a manner consistent with the terms of the gift or contract. Most frequently trustees are viewed as the guardians of the institution's assets, and in this respect the fiduciary duty often appears to be a restraint on actions that others see as necessary to fulfill the institution's ethical obligations. Examples would be the refusal of trustees to use a significant amount of institutional funds to build community housing or to incur losses in the endowment to express an opinion about the activities of companies in which it owns shares. It is useful to keep in mind, however, that trustees are charged with responsibility for the well-being of the entire institution and not simply its endowment and other monetary resources.

Increasingly in recent years, federal and state laws and regulations govern the activities of universities and provide a relatively clear basis for assessing the appropriateness of behavior. In some cases the law ties compliance to the receipt of federal funds, in others the federal or state standard governs regardless of any fiscal or other relationship with the government. Explicit legal obligations now heavily influence a wide range of university activity with important ethical ramifications, including affirmative action, research on human subjects, laboratory safety, and investigation of scientific misconduct. Actions or failures to act that two decades ago might have been the subject of legitimate differences of opinion are no longer so. Today the law provides a necessary point of reference and often dictates the answer to ethical questions the university confronts.

Having in mind these elements—the purposes of the university, its distinctive values, and its responsibilities and obligations—I would like to discuss a few issues with ethical dimensions that universities currently are considering and that raise important questions.

RELATIONS WITH INDUSTRY

The question of relationships between universities and industry is not a new one. For many years these relationships have taken a variety of forms as industry has sent people to universities for advanced training in business, science, and other fields, donated equipment and money and participated in programs, entered into consulting relationships with faculty members, and sponsored research. It is this last activity—the sponsorship of research—that has been the subject of particularly close scrutiny and considerable debate in recent years. The issue has been: should a private research university undertake industry-sponsored research and, if so, are there concerns that universities need to address and safeguards that should be in place to protect values important to universities?

There are those who would argue that the values of industry and of universities are so incompatible that a university truly concerned about its autonomy and integrity would decline to enter into research agreements with industry. Opponents of these agreements compare the danger allegedly posed by a "university-industrial complex" with that foreseen thirty years ago from the axis between industry and the military. It is argued that secrecy, the profit motive, and other characteristics commonly associated with industry will have a very damaging impact on the values of our universities.

Although it is clear that there are dangers, the case for industry-sponsored research at universities is very strong. The very purpose of the agreements mirrors a primary objective of a university: the discovery and transmission of knowledge. A prospective industrial sponsor, when approaching a university to undertake research, is asking it to do just what it is supposed to do. Moreover, the sponsor, by supplying the money to fund the research, is probably enabling the university to do something it could not otherwise do. The relationship can also foster the discovery of knowledge by enabling university researchers to benefit from the expertise, technical skills, and creativity of their industrial counterparts.

Public policy, as expressed in federal law, supports a research relationship between universities and industry. Congress has on several occasions strongly supported the idea that the national interest is served by the discovery, transmission, and exploitation of knowledge through industry-university cooperation. Thus, the industry-sponsored research is consistent not only with the university's own objectives but also with society's objectives as articulated in laws designed to provide guidance to universities as well as other institutions.

The dangers in the relationship are, however, real, and it is essential that universities forthrightly recognize these dangers and deal with them. The dangers arise primarily from the clash of values between the two cultures.

An important example of the difference in values relates to the issue of secrecy. Universities prize openness. They encourage the exchange of data and ideas. They consider the publication of research results to be both an individual right associated with academic freedom and an institutional obligation associated with the objective of a university as a discoverer and transmitter of knowledge. The rule is that whether to publish and what is to be published should be left to the individual and not dictated by others. Publication also subjects discovery to the marketplace of ideas—the results achieved by one scientist must stand up to the probing and testing and critical scrutiny of others. Because of this strong belief in openness and the right of the researcher to decide what is published, many universities, as a matter of principle, will not accept federally sponsored research that is classified.

Industry ordinarily operates on a different assumption. Research may ultimately benefit the public, but its initial purpose is almost always to benefit the company by creating and maintaining a competitive advantage. If this result is to be achieved, openness cannot be an operating principle. Rapid and complete transmission of knowledge through publication is likely to be at odds with the goal of competitive advantage.

In this dilemma—and it is a difficult one for many universities—there can be a strong temptation to compromise. The money is needed, and it is easy to rationalize that no great harm will occur if the sponsor has the right to edit a proposed publication to protect trade secrets or to delay publication for six or eight months to allow time for the sponsor to begin to exploit the research. After all, if restrictions are not accepted, the money may not be forthcoming and the research will not be accomplished.

Although this path has its understandable attractions, any significant compromises present an unacceptable risk. The risk is that universities will abandon a fundamental tenet, that they will slowly but inevitably lose their special role as discoverers and transmitters of knowledge for the benefit of all. By accepting restrictions on publication, a university is ceding institutional autonomy, restricting important rights of academic freedom, and insulating data and ideas from the test of the marketplace. These consequences transcend the interests of the particular institution and the individual researcher because they inevitably affect and ultimately weaken the entire academic enterprise.

Universities should, therefore, be alert and resistant to restrictions on publication that prevent the timely and complete dissemination of knowledge. Acceptance of this principle also serves the long-range interests of industry because universities that cease to maintain their unique characteristics are likely to lose their ability to make the unique contributions that industry seeks from its academic partners.

Relationships with industry can also be problematic for the individual researchers, presenting conflicts with their institution's and their own professional teaching and research values. A faculty member may end up a principal investigator on an industry-sponsored contract, a consultant to or director of a company, a shareholder, an advisory board member, or not infrequently in some combination of these relationships. The basic issue can be stated quite simply: because of the sometimes inconsistent values and interests of universities and industry, a faculty member may abandon or be perceived to be abandoning the values of a university teacher and researcher.

Some examples may help illustrate this point. A faculty member, when supervising the work of a graduate student, should be providing advice and direction on the basis of the intellectual value of the recommended research and the training needs of the student. The development and growth of the student should, in other words, be the paramount consideration. When a relationship with industry is present, there may be a tendency for the research needs and interests of the company to become important and possibly dominant factors, thereby distorting the teacher-student relationship and compromising a significant university value.

Secrecy can also be a large concern, even if the sponsored research agreement between a university and a company is properly crafted. Similar attention needs to be paid to any agreements between the company and a faculty member, whether for service as a consultant or as a member of an advisory board. Proper contractual provisions in institutional and individual agreements, although a necessary part of any university's attention to the issue of secrecy, do not, however, completely guard against the more subtle pressures that may exist. A faculty member with ties to industry is of necessity serving two masters whose interests may at times be not only different but also totally inconsistent. Trade secrets are, for example, an accepted part of one world and not of the other. It is the university's and faculty member's responsibility to be aware of this potential conflict and to understand that the primary commitment of the faculty member is to the university. This commitment requires that precedence be given to the values of the university and that the faculty member be diligent and act in good faith in all efforts to foster the flow of information into the public domain.

The good faith element is very important here, as it is in many areas of faculty conduct related to institutional values. The crucial decisions of when and what to publish cannot be successfully monitored by university or other authorities, nor should they be. Monitoring efforts would not succeed because they would be costly, time-consuming for all involved, and inconclusive. Publication decisions involve judgments that will vary according to temperament, experience, intellect, and other factors, and reasonable people will inevitably differ in many cases. Moreover, a review process on the timing and content of publications threatens another central university value: academic freedom. Academic freedom denotes the right of the faculty member engaged in research to reach his or her own publication decisions. These two considerations—review would be very difficult to accomplish and in any event it should not occur—place a special burden on faculty members to act in good faith. This strong obligation is a concomitant of the special freedom granted to academics.

Many of the same considerations that bear on the question of openness bear also on the issue of disinterestedness or objectivity. Universities in particular and society in general give researchers considerable latitude in determining how to plan and carry out their research, what conclusions to draw from their work, and what to publish or say about the results. Accompanying this grant of academic freedom is an expectation that the decisions made at the various stages in this continuum will be good faith decisions as little affected as possible by matters extraneous to the advancement and transmission of knowledge. In some respects, this area is difficult to police because many decisions are judgmental and certain extraneous considerations, such as personal advancement, may understandably enter the equation from time to time. The academic community, nevertheless, can and must have rules governing conflict of interest to give clear expression to the importance and the perception of objectivity. In relationships with industry, attention to objectivity can guide the behavior of a researcher who is a shareholder in the company sponsoring the research or in the company which hopes to market the drug that is being clinically tested under the researcher's direction and supervision.

Even in the absence of the possibility or likelihood of financial advantage, such as the clinical testing by the inventor of an unpatented medical device of little commercial value, the judgment of the researcher may be clouded by preconceptions and hope. Presumably it is for this reason that an important principle of experimental science is that the standard process for assessment requires replication of laboratory work by people not involved in the original research.

RACE RELATIONS

Thus far I have looked at concerns about a university's behavior that arise from its relationships with the outside world. Let me turn now to a different kind of test—one that principally reflects a conflict among internal values of the university. One of the most poignant of such conflicts arises from problems of race relations.

In the past few years many universities have experienced racial problems and controversies in one form or another. Reports from different parts of the country have informed us of physical and verbal confrontations, racial jokes on the radio, graffiti, disputes over presentation of classroom material, publication of articles with strong racial overtones, and other actions or forms of speech that have been the focus of attention and protest.

It is difficult to imagine an issue that is more closely related to the values of a university and deserving of attention. Race-based hostility has no place within a university community. The university should stand for the principles of individual dignity and respect for the individual without regard to race. Moreover, if the teaching and research objectives of a university are to be achieved, students and others should not suffer from an environment in which race-based hostility appears to be tolerated as an acceptable form of behavior. Such an environment interferes with the learning process by creating divisiveness in a pluralistic community and fear and insecurity in individuals, conveys the wrong message about values, and is detrimental to people of all races within the community. Finally, public policy and federal, state, and local laws that speak to the issue leave no doubt about the stated objectives of our society. A myriad of laws state that racial discrimination is illegal. The university, of all institutions, should be diligent in carrying out the letter and spirit of these laws.

There is, however, a dilemma that needs to be recognized and addressed by universities when dealing with issues of race relations. Freedom of expression, another value of great importance to the university, encompasses and protects speech that is nasty, uncivil, contrary to public policy and the stated objectives of the university, and scornful of basic university values. Free speech would be easy to defend in principle and in practice if deeply offensive speech were not thereby protected. Some opponents of racism or perceived racism on campuses have called for restrictions on expression of views. At Dartmouth, for example, there has been a demand that the *Dartmouth Review*, which was accused of publishing racist articles, be denied the same distribution rights that other publications have. The *New York Times* recently quoted a student at Stanford, where there have been several incidents with racial overtones, as saying, "We don't put as many restrictions on freedom of speech as we should." To heed those calls for limitations on speech would be a mistake.

Similarly, principles of academic freedom must be observed when dealing with issues of racism in the classroom. Academic freedom provides broad latitude for a faculty member's interpretation of the material and means of presenting it to students, and except in the most unusual cases, a university should hesitate to interfere with that freedom by imposing sanctions based on what a faculty member says in the classroom.

Race relations, in other words, requires a university to act in a way consistent with important institutional values that appear to lead to contrary results. Judgments have to be made as to what falls within the orbits of academic freedom or free speech and what constitutes unacceptable behavior that should be the subject of discipline. If the university is insensitive to this dilemma, it runs the risk of seeming to impose an orthodoxy that will not tolerate certain expressions of opinion, an orthodoxy that can easily extend beyond the issue of race relations. The university would also seem to be denying the view that the best remedy for the expression of bad ideas is the clear, forceful, and articulate expression of good ideas by faculty members, students, administrators, and others. This accepted remedy means that a university, although powerless to ban expressions of racism, has many ways of promoting racial understanding and respect that it can and should use.

CONCLUSION

Questions related to institutional values should be high on the agenda of research universities today. They are important, numerous, and frequently complex. The answers often are not obvious, and individual trustees, academics, students, and administrators who care deeply about their institutions will differ in their conclusions.

For three reasons the questions related to values need to be addressed internally. First, if the universities do not themselves satisfactorily address the issues, the government, and particularly the federal government, is likely to do so for them. Solutions imposed from the outside will be less sensitive to the needs of higher education in general and to the diversity found among individual institutions. By definition there will be a loss of institutional autonomy and quite possibly academic freedom, two central values of universities. Recent discussions in Washington concerning scientific misconduct illustrate the potential problems. From a pragmatic point of view it behooves universities to act.

Second, unlike the situation at some other times in this century, it is not the outside world that poses the threat to the values of universities. The problem is primarily internal. For example, there is often a question of balancing the need for additional dollars against the costs, in terms of sacrificing or compromising institutional values, of getting those dollars. Gifts from alumni and others with terms that interfere with institutional autonomy or academic freedom by specifying who will receive an appointment or the political or social views of prospective appointees, disregard of academic standards to the point of total abandonment in order to maintain a competitive big-time athletic program, sponsored research agreements that allow the sponsor to vet and edit publications to limit the extent and nature of transmission of research results—these are all situations in which, to a greater or lesser extent, the need for dollars has led to compromises. A university itself is in the best position to decide how to address its needs in light of its values. In other areas, where money is not the issue, the questions are often ones which can and should be resolved internally—policies concerning affirmative action, drugs and alcohol on campus, public safety, AIDS, shareholder responsibility, and free speech on campus. An issue like scientific misconduct is peculiarly within the competence of the academic community, which is in the best position to know how to keep misconduct to a minimum and how to make the crucial distinction between scientific error and scientific misconduct.

Third, universities function best when questions of values are identified, considered, and resolved by their own communities. Unless the university community recognizes that there is a problem, whether conflict of interest or racism, and that the problem is important and worthy of serious attention, it is unlikely that the issues will be thoroughly analyzed and understood or that any proposed solution will be properly tailored to solve the problem or thereafter observed in letter and spirit. The values of any community are developed and refined through internal discussion and reflection with the goal of arriving at a consensus, and universities are no different in this respect.

Consensus is not easy to achieve within universities today. The core of the university—the faculty—has become increasingly fractionated as universities and their schools and departments have become larger and larger, knowledge and disciplines have become more and more specialized, and extramural professional commitments have become increasingly important to some faculty members. Faculties are less cohesive and share fewer common understandings.

The challenge, therefore, is considerable. At a time when there is a lessened sense of community, universities should be addressing a series of important and complex issues related to their own values. The response of universities, and particularly their faculties, to this challenge will have a strong effect on their future role. At stake is whether they will continue to be vital and respected institutions making unique contributions to our society.

DONALD S. FREDRICKSON

VALUES AND THE ADVANCE

OF MEDICAL SCIENCE

We medical scientists, particularly those of us who are clinical investigators, have to keep in mind the peculiarities of our branch of the sciences. We emerged as a distinct profession not long before World War I, our numbers small and our art jejune. Suddenly we found ourselves in the forefront of a movement of all the sciences that was dramatically changing the scale of experimental inquiry in the United States. A brief experience (1941–1945) with wartime mobilization of scientific resources brought about a massive government investment in peacetime academic research and development.

It was a radical change. Only a few years before, many scientists and government officials had feared that public funding would be toxic to scientific freedom and irrevocably distort scientific values. Optimism soon replaced doubt, however, as the rapidly expanding and strengthened universities became a system for pursuing new knowledge that exceeded all predictions. Growth affected every discipline, but the life sciences expanded disproportionately. During this last half-century, biology has moved to center stage and medical science has won a special place in public attention. There is an insatiable public interest in the revelation of new ways to extend longevity or more powerful weapons against pain and disability.

Can such a popular prodigy as medical science do wrong? The answer to this question is yes. The principles, the goals, the very methods of weaving understanding from scientific knowledge are bound to the culture warp that supports, sets the tension, and gives overall direction to the enterprise. The experimentalists and their supporters have made a fateful bargain: trading continual negotiation of the underlying values for continued support.

The purpose of this essay is to examine how some values in medical science change and how the fundamental ones can be preserved during the interactions between the bodies politic and scientific. The vantage point selected is that of the National Institutes of Health, an agency that in the last half-century has been the principal mediator between the life sciences and the legislative and executive branches of the federal government.

THE EMERGING PROFESSION

When Lewellys Barker succeeded William Osler as professor of medicine at Johns Hopkins in 1905, he set up the first full-time research divisions in a clinical department in the United States.[1] An era of careful description of diseases was soon to be succeeded by scientific pursuit of their causes and treatment. Barker set up three laboratories along the functional lines of a model popular in Germany. The bacteriology laboratory was headed by Rufus Cole, who soon became the director of the first American hospital dedicated to clinical research established at the Rockefeller Institute in 1910. These events heralded the beginning of clinical investigation as a profession in America; but growth was slow, for few schools had full-time clinical faculties and investigations were limited.

Clinical investigation began to increase in the twenties but was of such a nature that it received a caustic appraisal by young Robert Loeb in his presidential address to the Young Turks in 1936. It "ran wild," he said, "recognizing no bounds, philosophical, intellectual, technical. . . . Medical students and young graduates, without consideration of 'Geist' or other qualifications, were urged to enter laboratories . . ." Loeb went on to note that a sobering result of the Great Depression was now the need for a hard appraisal to decide what was worthy of salvage out of this "great orgy."[2] The most vigorous clinical investigations at the time were in Germany, where chemistry had a strong industrial base and pharmaceutical trials often involved practices that brought about demands for development of a stronger ethical code. After considerable debate, new guidelines for innovative therapy and scientific experiments on man were issued by the German minister of the interior in 1931.[3]

In the United States, support for academic research at that time amounted to a few million dollars a year. Most of it came from private sources, mainly philanthropic foundations, and was distributed to relatively few institutions. Government funds for university research amounted to a few hundred thousand dollars. Young scientists without private means had a hard time getting support for a career in academic science.

Imminent Change

Very few of the professors or their penurious apprentices in the teaching hospitals in the early 1930s could have had an inkling of the powerful tonic being prepared for an anemic medical science. To be sure, the preparations were under way in an unlikely place, the sleepy southern capital city of Washington, D.C. The ringleaders were a handful of physicians who did not represent the elite of academic medicine. Most of them had gone directly into the United States Public Health Service upon graduation from medical school or after a year of internship. But they had a vision that the contents of the doctor's bag could be made much more useful.

NIH and NCI Are Born

After smoldering for about ten years, and then accompanied by a memorable burst of rhetoric, the "Cancer War" broke out in the Congress in 1937.[4] The newly established National Cancer Institute joined its older sibling, the National Institute of Health (1930), which had been established in 1887 as the Laboratory of Hygiene of the Marine Hospital Service, the precursor of the U.S. Public Health Service.[5] The years of debate and redrafting of the proposals of Senator Homer Ransdall of Louisiana to create the NIH had slowly sensitized other members of the Congress to the promise of a government-backed effort to gain more fundamental understanding of the diseases that plagued the country. Despite advances in preventing contagion and the arrival of the sulfa drugs, pneumonia, tuberculosis, syphilis, and other venereal diseases were still serious problems in America. As infant mortality declined, people were living longer and the incidence of cardiovascular diseases, mental illness, cancer, and other chronic diseases increased.

Tommy's Troops

Very few of today's biomedical scientists know the name of the single most effective person behind the projection of the NIH into the center of the world of biomedical science. He was Thomas Parran, in the front ranks of the many surgeons general of the Public Health Service. Parran, born in 1892, was a 1915 graduate of Georgetown University Medical School. He joined the Public Health Service two years later and in doing his stint of fieldwork came to the attention of Surgeon General Hugh Cumming. Governor Franklin D. Roosevelt of New York asked Cumming in 1930 to suggest someone to fill the post of state health officer in Albany. Parran was chosen and in the relaxed era of the thirties he was able to take the post and remain in the service. Several years later, he took part in an important study requested of the National Academy by President Roosevelt, a review of the medical research in the Public Health Service. The inquiry was conducted by Simon Flexner, Milton J. Rosenau, who was a former director of the Hygienic Laboratory, and Parran, the trio acting as a subcommittee of the Science Advisory Board.[6] Their report advocated increased research on chronic diseases, especially through a strengthening of the NIH. Congress authorized the support they requested, but no new funds were appropriated. Nevertheless, the NIH thereby became linked to other New Deal social legislation and caught the eye of the administration and the Congress.

When Cumming's term as surgeon general ended in 1936, President Roosevelt thought of his state health officer as the replacement. By then Parran was considered an excellent administrator and was well known for his candid views on venereal disease prevention—he had been cut off a national radio network and replaced by a piano for uttering the forbidden word *syphilis*. Parran also nursed a compelling urge to start a war on chronic diseases, before most experts felt we knew enough about biology to begin. His preparations over the next twelve years left few details unattended. He chose promising officers like Norman Topping, Leonard Scheele, and Mark Hollis to plan with him. As chair of the National Advisory Health Council and of the National Advisory Cancer Council, he tested the opinions of leading medical scientists and public health figures. He worked with Congressman Alfred Lee Bulwinkle, a thirteen-term congressman from North Carolina, to bring a chaotic series of prior Public Health authorities into a single bill (the Public Health Service Act, PL 78-410), signed on July 1, 1944. This act gave the Service, and particularly NIH, remarkably broad authority to conduct research.

Many of the events of that extraordinary ten years between 1937 and 1946 have now been described in rich detail.[7] They include the mobilization of the nation's scientific resources under the Office of Scientific Research and Development (OSRD) by Dr. Vannevar Bush during World War II. A part of OSRD was the Committee on Medical Research (CMR), which oversaw more than 250 contracts supporting medical research in universities, industries, and independent research institutes. As the eventual victory of the Allies became certain, OSRD prepared to close down. Bush was urged by the president and others to reconsider, and in a valedictory report he proposed the formation of a National Research Foundation to continue government support for research in the private sector. The small committee of medical academicians whose advice and support were sought by Bush agreed that government support should be continued, but they wanted a separate organization for medical research, more on the lines of one the British had put together before World War I which was given a royal charter as the Medical Research Council in 1920.

The gestation of what would eventually become the National Science Foundation became intolerably prolonged. First there was competing legislation (the Kilgore Bill) to form a government research organization with centralized planning and stiff government control over patents on inventions, a concept alien to Bush. Then Congress was diverted by the necessity of erecting an Atomic Energy Commission to keep a lock on the newly revealed destructive power of atomic fission. As time dragged on with no replacement for OSRD, Rolla Eugene Dyer, the Public Health Service member on the Committee on Medical Research, wrote A. N. Richards, the chair, to remind him that under PL 78-410 the Public Health Service had the authorities required to take over the role of the CMR. There was a long silence before the CMR, anxious to fold its tents, held a last meeting in 1945. The members from the other government agencies, the army and the navy, evinced no interest as Richards offered up the contracts still outstanding. Only Gene Dyer raised his hand, quietly picked up the lot one by one, and took them home to Bethesda. Later there was a presidential veto over the proposed authority of the National Science Foundation director before that agency was born in 1950. Its initial authorization was fifteen million dollars. The supplemental appropriation for NIH to renew those first OSRD contracts—renamed grants—had brought the total NIH grant appropriations for fiscal year 1947 to a majestic 850,000 dollars. By 1950 the appropriation had soared to over fifty million dollars. Stephen Strickland sums up the achievement: "Especially in hindsight can we see what a stunning feat Dr. Parran and Dr. Dyer performed, through ingenuity and persistence, in moving from a modest existing program to the building of a medical research empire, simply by arranging the takeover of a handful of wartime research contracts and converting them into ongoing grants."[8]

Over the dozen years of Parran's tenure as surgeon general (1936–1948) there were several others in the Public Health Service who especially deserve recognition as founders of the modern NIH. Dr. Lewis R. Thompson, whom everyone called Jimmy, was a remarkably resourceful man who, long before he became director of NIH in 1937, had been engaged in activities designed to change the NIH into a "major medical machine" to fight chronic diseases. Indeed, his enthusiasm for expansion was deeply disturbing to more conservative colleagues, including his predecessor as NIH director, the world-renowned leprosy expert, Dr. George McCoy.[9] As an aide to Cumming, Thompson had been at the elbow of Senator Ransdell as the legislation for creation of NIH was steered through the Congress. It was also Thompson who arranged to slip Parran aboard the 1932 subcommittee of the august Science Advisory Committee, an act said to have greatly angered the National Academy of Sciences because Parran was not one of its members. NIH owes its present location to Thompson. His numerous connections in Washington enabled him to learn that a large tract of land in Bethesda, a pastoral suburb of Washington, had been offered as a gift to the government, but that no department had bothered to respond. Jimmy drafted a letter and managed to have it conveyed to the president for his signature, thanking the owners for giving their land to the National Institutes of Health.[10] The cornerstone of Building 1 was laid June 30, 1938.

Dyer, Parran's other partner, was outwardly more retiring than the gregarious Thompson. Director of NIH from 1942 to 1950, he was very much the introspective laboratory scientist in appearance. Hidden beneath this guise, however, were formidable diplomatic talents, a stubborn streak, and strong scientific values. When Dyer found himself the possessor of sixty or so expiring Office of Scientific Research and Development contracts—the seedlings from which a mighty forest was to spring—he enlisted the help of another Public Health officer, Dr. Cassius J. Van Slyke. Van Slyke's previous experience was venereal disease control. Guided by Dyer, and with the help of Ernest Allen, a former schoolteacher, Van Slyke took the responsibility for nurturing the roots of the NIH extramural program in its first several years.

The Clinical Center

Concurrent with the new grants program, the Public Health Service made a second daring move. The intent to build a large research hospital at Bethesda was set out in Parran's plans for the postwar NIH drawn up by 1944.[11] Therefore, barely a year after getting the fateful supplemental appropriation renewing the first OSRD contracts, Dyer was back before the appropriations committee describing the need for much more money to build not just a hospital, but one solely for research, and the largest such ever conceived. The House labor and health appropriations subcommittee, especially its chairperson Frank B. Keefe of Wisconsin, enthusiastically accepted the rationale: "From such a close association of fundamental and applied clinical research should arise a new type of scientific worker who is schooled in the exacting methods and disciplined thinking of the fundamental research man and who at the same time is a physician."[12]

The extent to which the Clinical Center proposition was widely considered by the academic community to be premature—even presumptuous—may be inferred from the comments of an eminent researcher in 1950: "No clinical research has been undertaken in the fields of cancer, tuberculosis, or mental illness, since the [Rockefeller] Institute believes that basic laboratory research has not advanced far enough to make possible clinical studies."[13]

There was other criticism in both the Congress and the academic community, but by 1948 the ground had already been broken, and in 1951, when I came for a recruitment interview, the hull of the giant unfinished ship already loomed over the landscape at Bethesda. The million and four hundred thousand gross square feet of the new hospital included accommodations for five hundred research patients wrapped in a thousand laboratories. The cost was thirty-seven million (1953) dollars. The first patients were admitted in 1953.

Such a hospital might have been impossible to staff in ordinary times. The intramural research staff of NIH were nearly all basic scientists except for temporary clinical units for cancer at Boston and Baltimore. Once again, however, the Public Health Service leaders were favored by historical coincidence. Before the doors of the Clinical Center opened, the Korean War erupted, and the call sounded for the second physician draft in ten years. The Clinical Center was qualified to provide Selective Service credit to a limited number of physicians seeking training as medical scientists. The hospital was soon fully staffed with a large number of the next generation of American medical academicians.

THE BASIC VALUES

Knowledge is a perpetually unfinished mosaic. Scientists purchase the rights to contribute to it by conforming to the internal ethos of scientific inquiry. Although it may seem complex, this code rests on two major requirements. One is scrupulous recognition of priority in contributions. The second is open submission of evidence supporting a scientific conclusion for judgment and confirmation by one's peers. The code is universal and allows an intensely competitive world community to govern interactions among its members and protect the quality of the knowledge mosaic. Rash attempts by society to change these intrinsic values risk disabling a mechanism of incalculable value to civilization.

The autonomy of scientists, which is the essence of their claim to a profession,[14] is also hostage to certain extrinsic values derived from the culture in which they work. These values may be subject to change. After the war, the agreement between government and science that was inherent in the NIH research grant program bound the movement of the shuttlecock of medical science much more tightly to this culture warp.

With one or two exceptions, the scientific values declaimed by the founders of the NIH extramural program at its inception were not new. These intrinsic values had been carried to America by several generations of scientists who had learned them in British or Continental laboratories in the nineteenth century. If there was any difference in their expression it would come from a rude American lack of regard for Old World academic and professorial tradition. The transfer of older values to a new milieu in which individual scientists were given government research grants was characterized by unusual freedom and autonomy for young American researchers.

As the NIH took over the medical research program, the Office of Scientific Research and Development—or more specifially its Committee on Medical Research component—served as the prime example of how things should be done. The OSRD emphasized the selecting of scientists, rather than institutions per se. NIH continued this practice ever more religiously. Don K. Price says that it was because Congress wanted it to be this way.[15] Congress, he writes, wanted to avoid the thorny choices inherent in favoring one institution over another. Many of the universities, for example, were sectarian in origin, and uncomfortable constitutional issues could be raised. So Congress delegated the decisions to the scientists. If the results turned out unhappily, they could always recall the delegations. OSRD had also depended upon groups of well-known scientists to decide upon the priority and the quality of the applications, thus substituting expert peer review for local university decision. There was also a minimum of government interference with the scientists, in either their allocations or their research.

Within the first year of the NIH grants program, some 250 leading medical scientists had been enlisted to serve on study sections. Van Slyke was speaking for all the NIH leaders when he wrote that it was "a medical research program of scientists and by scientists." He considered that the program and the scientific method rested "on the integrity and independence of research workers, and their freedom from control, regimentation, and outside interference."[16]

There was one change. As far as many scientists were concerned, the war on chronic diseases had to concentrate first on accumulating more knowledge of basic physiology and biochemistry. Dyer echoed these sentiments: ". . . emphasis is placed not upon the goal, but upon the scientist pursuing interest[s] as distinct from bureaucratic control over those interests."[17]

James A. Shannon, who came to NIH in 1950 at the invitation of Van Slyke to be the director of intramural research in the National Heart Institute, was a first-class scientist and administrator, whose reign as director of NIH extended from 1955 to 1968. Shannon was a powerful source of exegesis of the science-oriented manner in which the partnership was developing. He had strong, almost Manichean views of research values, ones that we all emulated: "Selection of good men and good ideas—and the rejection of the inferior—is the key. All subsequent administrative actions having to do with the adjustment of budgets, and so forth, are essentially trivial in relation to this basic selection process." [18]

In those early days, *excellence* was the word for the highest value. It included not only technical proficiency but the intrinsic imperatives of respect for the laws of evidence, priority rights, and agreement to faithful reporting in only those journals employing rigorous review. Excellence meant being highly rated by one's peers. Excellence, above all, was good science as opposed to bad.

The sentiments did not always please citizen activists who had helped Congress add an institute for heart disease after the one for cancer, then one for dental problems, another for arthritis, and for mental health—progenitors of a list that continues to grow today. With an eye for balancing the tensions, however, Congress had already provided for on-line protection of the public's interest in the research by seeing to it that each new institute had an advisory council, including laypeople. They were fitted with the power to approve the grants awarded by the study sections, but the practical purpose of these bodies was to see that the public's preoccupation with the utilitarian function wasn't forgotten by the research community.

EMERGENCE OF NEW VALUES

In the context within which NIH was being shaped by its scientific and public partners, several new values emerged as important subjects of debate and defense. The first was that of the integral nature of biomedical research. From 1937 on, NIH was a growing collection of institutes that derived their support and unswerving mandates from the anxiety of many who are victims of or who fear one particular disease. The structure of NIH has always been subjected to high centrifugal forces. Parran recognized this tendency to scatter early and saw to it that PL 78-410 erased any separatist status of the National Cancer Institute and made it a division of NIH. Later Parran and Dyer had to struggle quietly and diplomatically for years to outwit the desires of the Cancer Institute and the Mental Health sympathizers to put up separate research hospitals and thus Balkanize biomedical research on the NIH campus.[19]

The preservation of a wholeness of inquiry in biology and medicine would from time to time be a major source of tension at NIH. Early on, another persistent source became the division of resources among differing kinds of research. All the OSRD orientation toward utilitarian research could not be eliminated. The differences between categorical research and basic research became almost conflicting extrinsic values. The former meant, at first, disease-oriented research, then targeted or applied or directed research. Early on, basic research was idealized by most scientists as the independent pursuit of knowledge without commitment to its relevance. It also has always meant freedom to go into molecular dimensions. Nowadays, however, when molecular genetics is the basis for an industrial pursuit of a portion of an HIV gene for the purpose of making a vaccine, the targeting of the task or its relevance to disease no longer detracts from the respectability. Utilitarian research has lost pejorative connotation. This does not mean, however, that, with respect to protecting the capacity for basic research, all the tension normally surrounding the setting of priorities has gone away. Basic research has come to mean those activities essential to the training of new scientists, for whom a period of autonomous, self-directed research is considered an essential rite of passage to the status of independent investigators. Likewise a certain number of the best independent investigators have to be retained in autonomous, fundamental research in order to maintain the sharpness of the cutting edge of science. The practical manifestation of basic research has long been the traditional research project grant (the RO-1 grant, in NIH parlance). The last decade has been a period in which the protection of the capacity to award annually a minimum number of RO-1 grants is the sheet anchor of the annual NIH budget process. But this period may be ending and the negotiation of priorities may soon require new definitions, if not new values.

Another view of what is or is not categorical occurred in a short-lived revolt against NIH led by some academicians in 1955. At that time Oveta Culp Hobby, the first secretary of Health, Education, and Welfare, called upon the National Science Foundation to make an outside study of the research conducted by her department. The special committee convened for this purpose was a group of university scientists led by C. N. H. Long, the dean of the Yale medical school. To the ire of NIH leadership, the committee recommended that the NIH extramural program be severed from the intramural program. Their argument was that the direction was too categorical and that the desired mode was "unrestricted institutional grants" to universities, which should also include teaching grants to the schools.[20] The new secretary of HEW, Marion Folsom, was unmoved. He appointed his own review committee, headed by Dr. Stanhope Bayne-Jones (another dean of Yale). The Senate, equally disturbed, asked Dr. Boisfeuillet Jones to conduct his own study of the recommendation. Both of these reviews disagreed with the NSF special committee. Its report was never published.

CHANGING VALUES IN CLINICAL INVESTIGATION

When the Clinical Center opened, its medical board issued rules for clinical investigation. Self-experimentation was forbidden, although one might seek permission of the NIH director for an exception. The formulation and conduct of research were the direct responsibility of the principal investigator who had admitted the patient, and any research procedures deviating from accepted medical practice or involving unusual hazards required group consideration. The rules further noted that determination of what was considered to be unusual was to be "on an individual basis, in the light of total experience developed in well-recognized institutions accepted by the profession for the excellence of their staff in conducting medical care and research."[21]

Some of what "well-recognized institutions" accepted as standards for treatment of human volunteers in 1953 would not stand the passage of time. Rothman has recently observed succinctly that "the CMR gave the NIH not only its organizational framework, but its ethos as well."[22] He described examples of clinical research conducted under CMR contracts that appeared to undercut the protection of human subjects because, "in philosophical terms, wartime inevitably promoted utilitarian over absolutist provisions." CMR experiments included immunization studies of different captive groups, some being children in orphanages or others in institutions for the mentally retarded, and the induction of malaria in prisoner volunteers.

Not only in those studies, but in many elsewhere, the procurement of informed consent and considerations of risk/benefit were irregular and poorly documented. These practices did not begin to change materially in many institutions until the 1960s. By 1964 NIH was supporting about fifteen hundred clinical research projects in some two thousand research beds, including the five hundred in the Clinical Center. The intramural program had engaged in studies involving more than one thousand prisoner volunteers and two thousand normal subject volunteers, and the amount of clinical investigation was continuing to expand as the annual budget of NIH exceeded its 1945 level by more than six hundred fold. Experts in ethics and allied disciplines were giving increased attention to the mores of clinical investigation, and several international bodies issued statements of principles.

Dissemination of NIH Rules

In 1963, the surgeon general requested a survey of existing codes for clinical research. The results of the survey were reported to the director of NIH in the following year. The text included the following summary of opinions obtained both from within NIH and from outside advisors who had been consulted:

> For a variety of reasons, then, it would be advantageous to the national health research program if any general guidelines or code of clinical research behavior were developed by a non-federal body, preferably by a body enjoying the highest professional respect . . . It would add to existing insecurities if the NIH were to assume an exclusive or authoritarian position concerning the definition of ethical boundaries or conditions mandatory for clinical research.[23]

The founders of the NIH extramural program had taken great pains to avoid any semblance of authoritarianism or excessive government bureaucracy. They had an equally strong desire that the intramural program should be accepted as a part of the great academic world of research. Fearful of any animosity, they kept intramural scientists off the study sections for a number of years. David Price explained the reason:

> One of the things that we were always sensitive about and Dr. Dyer felt very strongly about, was that the grants program ought not to be run by the intramural scientists at the NIH . . . That was the easy way to go . . . [but] to do that would place the program in some jeopardy, with people feeling that their ideas were being "stolen" by government scientists. We wanted to keep any accusation of that kind from occurring, so we chose to use outside reviewers.[24]

This commendable mind-set can be considered one of the reasons why NIH has managed to stay philosophically in harmony with the academic scientific community to the present day. Another reason, of course, is that the intramural program then became the training ground for so many who later have gone to the universities.

There can be a negative side, however, to too much deference on the part of NIH in working with the academic community. It is not always appreciated how close NIH has come on occasion to being saddled with cumbersome regulatory mandates incompatible with a great scientific agency. Those threats have generally occurred when the academic community has been perceived as responding sluggishly to cries for examination and possible adjustment of its scientific values. Indeed, in the interests of maintaining the crucial partnership intact, it is incumbent upon an NIH director to sense when nonfederal academic bodies have taken unduly long to respond. The penalty for misjudgment here can be the sudden arrival of new constraints from an unsympathetic and possibly uncomprehending authority.

With respect to standards for clinical investigation, the NIH director apparently felt in 1964 that he could wait no longer to adjust values in relation to in-house clinical research. Dr. Shannon appointed an intramural ad hoc committee in 1964 and charged it to update the 1953 Clinical Center rules with respect to therapeutic and nontherapeutic research on patients and experiments on normal volunteers.[25] Actually his order went to the late Dr. Jack Masur, the physician whom Parran had induced to come to Bethesda to design the Clinical Center in 1947, and who was now its director. I was one of the members of the small group chosen by Masur to meet periodically for more than a year. I recall my naïve initial reaction to Masur's proposal that our legal counsel would participate as a member of the group. I shared a then general opinion of scientists that laypeople could not be expected to understand the experimental procedures and therefore could not properly weigh issues of risk and benefit. The counsel promptly asked me what legal defense I would employ if a patient claimed to have been injured in an experiment that could not conceivably benefit the patient, no matter how much benefit accrued to others. My preceptors had all tacitly shared the belief that, provided one obeyed the ethos of Hippocrates, the hope of benefit to humanity permitted exploration of the unknown with the patient's permission. That such a license would be worthless in court was a shocking revelation. Of course, by 1964, very few judicial tests had clarified the legal status of clinical research, but I count this conversation as an unforgettable sample of the greening of a generation of American clinical investigators in the 1960s.

Our committee sent its report to Shannon in early 1966. In July, the Public Health Services extended the updated Clinical Center practices for group review of clinical research to all grantee institutions, requiring them to "utilize groups of associates, established at the institution to provide competent, independent review . . . and to ascertain the adequacy of provisions for protecting the rights and welfare of human subjects in research, the appropriateness of the methods used to secure informed consent, and the risks and potential benefits" of every research project.[26] Later that year an incendiary paper by Henry E. Beecher of the Massachusetts General Hospital appeared, citing over twenty examples of clinical experimentation published in 1964 that he considered unethical. Three of the examples used by Beecher came from the NIH intramural program.[27]

Some clinical scientists complained that the extension of the Clinical Center rules to all institutions was the beginning of the end of clinical investigation in the United States. Many more, however, realized that changes were overdue to protect patients and investigators alike. It was an inevitable move, one that proved that the scientific community, with the help of NIH, could make important adjustments in extrinsic values without requiring the prior intervention of Congress or the administration.

Government Intervention

The implementation of the 1966 rules, however, eventually caused reactions that stimulated Congress to become highly interested in the ethics of clinical investigation. The rules had stipulated that, after examining new projects, institutions must then proceed to look at the rules of conduct in older, still active projects. It was during this audit that the Tuskegee project, which involved the withholding of therapy for syphilis, came to light in 1971.[28]

About this same time Senator Edward M. Kennedy became chairman of the Senate Health Subcommittee and began numerous hearings on the ethics of research and on the ethics of health care such as sterilization of women. Kennedy then proposed the creation of a freestanding regulatory commission, operating outside the Public Health Service grant-awarding agencies, to regulate biomedical ethics. The comparable subcommittee in the House of Representatives was opposed to the creation of a new external overseer of the ethics of clinical investigation, and a compromise was finally reached. The Senate committee stipulated that, if NIH would prepare and the Public Health Service would release new regulations for the protection of human subjects, *and* if the Senate committee found them satisfactory, the proposal for the new commission would be withdrawn. The regulations were drawn in record time and satisfied the Senate committee. After opportunity for public review and comment, the regulations were published on May 30, 1974.[29] The House bill, an amendment of the Public Health Service Act to establish training awards as well as "to provide for the protection of human subjects involved in biomedical and behavioral research," became law six weeks later. It has been observed that this was one of the very rare examples of the virtue of approving the rules *prior* to passage of the law requiring them.[30]

The First Proscriptions of Research

Title II of the new law established a national advisory commission (the first of several ethics commissions) to prepare guidelines for research involving human subjects, including research involving living fetuses. It included a section 213 which read:

> Until the Commission has made its recommendations to the Secretary pursuant to section 202(b), the Secretary may not conduct

or support research in the United States or abroad on a living human fetus, before or after the induced abortion of such fetus, unless such research is done for the purpose of assuring the survival of such fetus.

This proscription of research appears to have been the second since the establishment of the NIH. A section of the Public Health Service Act earlier in the 1970s had prohibited Public Health Service grantees from carrying out any research on abortifacients. (This prohibition is now annually extended to all federal grantees and contractors under the Hyde amendment attached to each appropriation bill.)

Proscription of research is without question one of the most sobering value shifts in any discipline of science. Of course, genuine concerns can rise to such a point that there is no choice but to halt research until the issues have been aired and decisions about proceeding carefully made. When the concerns are ideological in origin, however, the barriers erected may be exceedingly difficult to lower again, and gaping holes of ignorance in an area of the mosaic of knowledge are left neglected. Moreover, if the proscribed area of research involves scientific inquiry into procedures which are simultaneously allowed to continue as matters of medical practice, the best interests of society may be severely compromised.

The National Commission for the Protection of Human Subjects of Biomedical and Behavioral Research (sometimes known as the Ryan Commission after its able chairman, Dr. Kenneth J. Ryan) gave its first report on time in May 1975. The commission recommended that fetal research proceed as long as the Institutional Review Board (IRB, now mandated for each hospital receiving any HEW funds under the Public Health Service Regulations) determined that the risk to the fetus was minimal. (The test of minimal risk implies that the risk to a fetus about to be aborted can be no greater than that which is permissible for a fetus that is to be carried to term.) This portion of their recommendation was incorporated into regulations in August 1975, and the regulation contained the requirement that an ethics advisory board be convened to review and approve any experiment in which an IRB judges the minimum risk rule is exceeded.[31]

The charter for such an ethics advisory board was initiated at the end of the tenure of HEW secretary David Mathews and revised by his successor, Joseph A. Califano, Jr., in 1978. Secretary Califano convened the first (and only) such board in 1978, in order that it might consider a grant application for the study of in-vitro fertilization that had been approved by an NIH study section. The board approved the application, provided the purpose of the experiments was to promote procreation by the donors involved. Secretary Califano left office abruptly in July 1979, before he could accept the board's recommendation. The next secretary, Patricia Roberts Harris, elected not to implement this decision and neither have her successors in the succeeding eight years. The charter of the Ethics Advisory Board has since lapsed. Absence of a board constitutes a de facto moratorium on all research on in-vitro fertilization and all procedures that create more than minimal risk for fetuses.

Another stalemate presently exists in the question of the transplantation of tissue from fetal remains. This procedure is not covered by the 1975 regulations per se. However, those regulations and other laws do tangentially affect the decision for they require that the mother of the fetus be healthy, in effect making her a research subject as well. There are also the requirements of applicable laws, such as the national organ transplant law and the uniform anatomical gift acts of several states, under which maternal consent (and provided the father does not dissent) to the use of fetal tissue is required. A request to use fetal tissue for transplantation was approved in December 1988 by the advisory committee to the director, NIH, after a subcommittee selected to represent a full spectrum of views on the subject agreed by a wide majority. This recommendation has so far not been acted upon at the level of the assistant secretary for health.

RESEARCH PERCEIVED AS A THREAT
TO PUBLIC SAFETY

There have been other threats of proscription. None has equaled the furious demands in 1973, and for several years thereafter, for the proscribing of an entire field of research when genetic engineering raised cries of imminent damage to public safety and the global environment. Two separate views bear witness; the opening of a 1977 House resolution introduced by Richard Ottinger (Dem., N.Y.): "Whereas unregulated research involving recombinant DNA is potentially devastating to the health and safety of the American people . . . ," contrasted with the words of Stanford University professor of biology, Dr. Charles Yanofsky, in a letter to the director of NIH: "I personally believe that if either of the current bills on recombinant DNA research is passed in its present form, research in the biomedical sciences will be plunged into a period comparable to the Dark Ages when inquiry was prohibited. This would come about despite the absence of any evidence that recombinant DNA research is harmful . . . ."[32]

It is noteworthy that two of the greatest paradigmatic shifts in physics and biology nearly overlapped in time. It was less than a decade between the discovery of atomic fission (1934) and the elucidation of DNA as the substance that carries genetic information (1943). Ten years later, the downside of fission emerged with the explosion of the atomic bomb. Subsequently there continued a series of brilliant episodes in the story of DNA, most notably the discovery of the structure of the gene (1954) and the later demonstration that genes could be cut and spliced enzymatically (the early 1970s).

This latter discovery of the means to recombine genetic material abruptly initiated a most dramatic change in biology, offering to the world a view of life in molecular dimensions heretofore undreamed of. We can now look back with amazement at the change in horizon that these technologies have made, but we should not forget that the early proposals to exploit them were so frightening that scientists considered disowning the new power. Some scientists seized the occasion to describe a population of chimeras creeping from the site of crossing of forbidden genetic boundaries, dangerous fantasies which the media dutifully compounded. Some critics hastened to compare the dilemma of the meddlesome biologists to the unhappy retrospection of nuclear physicists after Alamogordo.

On their own, the biomedical researchers most familiar with the new technology declared a pause in using it until agreement could be found on how to proceed. The NIH was asked by the scientists to provide a venue and leadership in developing guidelines for the research. The secretary of HEW chartered the Recombinant Advisory Committee (appropriately nicknamed the "rack"), consisting of experts on recombination technology from around the country and chaired by the NIH director of intramural research. Initially, there was one lay member, a political scientist. Subsequently the composition of the RAC would undergo several revisions. With each, the mixture of molecular biologists and other scientific experts with representatives of other professions became richer. This opportunity to compress the deliberations of arcane scientific matter by experts and laypersons sitting together would eventually provide a model for governing this very field in a responsible and effective way.

The guidelines were finally sent to NIH at the end of 1975. Their arrival was accompanied by a poisonous cloud of fear and passionate hostility. The scientific community was not unified. Some, scorning the need for guidelines, wanted to go on as before. A minority of scientists were so alarmed as to argue for banning the use of the techniques of genetic engineering. The majority of the scientists at first watched and then reacted responsibly and effectively in the nearly three years of debate that followed. Numerous environmentalist organizations soon had teams in Washington to follow each move of the NIH. There were forums at which doomsayers proclaimed "they would not be cloned" and the media surpassed themselves with tales of imaginary hazards. The crowds observing the proceedings included industrialists anxious to capitalize upon the new prospects for biotechnology, lawyers representing clients of opposite persuasions, and numerous staff members from the Congress and executive branch.

NIH initially sought—and fortunately obtained the backing of the HEW general counsel to do so—that, above all else, the exploration of such uncharted scientific territory must be undertaken with issuance of guidelines, not rule making. Guidelines could be changed as the experts determined it was safe to do so. Once in place, regulations could easily cause the state of understanding of hazards and potential to remain frozen indefinitely or even to require central review and approval of laboratory experiments across the nation. But the price of keeping the values under the control of the scientific community was to make every step of the way a highly public affair. We proceeded from there almost by parliamentary procedure, with every meeting open, announced beforehand, leaving no opportunity for claims that science was attempting an end run.

Therefore, a dramatic series of public hearings on the guidelines was prepared before their release. It was most unusual, because NIH directors had promulgated guidelines without fanfare before, and not all scientists appreciated this new turn of events. The Director's Advisory Committee (DAC) provided the only chartered body suitable for use, and its membership was quickly augmented with representatives of most of the prevailing biases. There were students, technicians working in molecular genetics laboratories, holders of Nobel prizes, a federal judge, the president's adviser on consumer affairs, environmentalists, dissident scientists, the president of the National Academy of Sciences, and regulators, among others. The hearings confirmed that the temperatures of the body scientific and of the body politic were high. The proscription would have to be sustained until a careful process could be fashioned to lift it. Most notably, neither at this nor at any other of the public hearings was what was most eagerly sought ever heard: reliable information that increased the hazards above the previous speculations. The hearings, however, proved beneficial in providing opportunity for ventilation.

A determined effort was also made from the first to keep a full public record. All the proceedings, letters, comments, and other communications were indexed and bound. The archive continued long past the crises and by May 1986 filled ten volumes.

Powerful regulatory agencies (Environmental Protection Agency, Food and Drug Administration, National Institute of Occupational Health and Safety, Occupational Safety and Health Agency, Center for Disease Control, and Department of Transportation) at first claimed jurisdiction. Through the HEW secretary, the NIH requested the president to charter a government-wide committee to permit all the agencies seeking regulatory authority and all the agencies likely to support research in the techniques (National Science Foundation, Department of Agriculture, Veterans Administration, Alcohol, Drug Abuse, Mental Health Administration, Department of Energy, and Department of Defense) to iron out the competing claims of authorities and to reach agreement to use a single set of guidelines. This Interagency Recombinant DNA Committee speedily reached a consensus that no agency had clear regulatory authority over this kind of research, and NIH was able to retain primary responsibility for what was to come. From time to time, cries arose for NIH to use existing regulatory authority. One of these was to resort to an obscure section 361 of the Public Health Service Act which allowed the secretary to seize control of any agents capable of threatening the public with an infectious disease. The secretary agreed with us that no one had proved that an epidemic would be caused by this research.

The NIH guidelines for recombinant DNA research were promulgated in the summer of 1976, despite the threat of environmentalists to enjoin the government because it had not filed an environmental impact statement in compliance with the National Environmental Policy Act. NIH had to take a calculated risk and concluded that the risk of prosecution for defiance of NEPA was outweighed by the crumbling willingness of the scientists to stay away from their benches. Then an NIH task force fell to preparing an environmental impact statement. The task took months as scientists fought HEW bureaucrats over how one should rank risks that were theoretical. The heavy tome bearing the statement, however, proved to be worth its weight in supporting the government's case in court. Injunctions which had been sought to stop the research were eventually denied.

Within the 1977 session of Congress, no fewer than twelve bills were introduced which proposed some kind of statutory control of laboratory experiments in this most complex area. Some stipulated fines of tens of thousands of dollars a day for violation of a guideline. One bill proposed the establishment of an external commission of part-time members, only a few of whom would be permitted to be experts in molecular genetics. The commission was to regulate all recombinant DNA research and, in its spare time, debate the ethical issues involved. Several states also proposed laws to add state control to federal and arguments over preemption echoed through the halls. Hearings went on for more than a year.

The eventual outcome, as most everyone knows, was a felicitous one. No laws were passed, the guidelines were accepted by industry and other nongovernmental researchers; along with guidelines used by Britain, the NIH guidelines became the major source of guidance for the rest of the world. Above all, time lost in exploiting the new technologies was not so long that we had to forfeit a steadily growing beneficence of new understanding.

In summing up this sketchy description of a tumultuous period, one may list some of the ingredients that helped the scientific community to prove that it is basically a self-regulating system. NIH was called upon early enough in the rDNA period so that it could forego its traditional shyness in helping orchestrate an exercise of value setting. The agency was able to mobilize the scientific community to provide the experts (the Recombinant Advisory Committee) and, at the same time, speedily open to the public the deliberations of the experts and an explanation of their meaning to the various audiences at interest (the Director's Advisory Committee). From its bipolar nature, NIH also had access both to the executive branch (the president, the secretary of HEW, the Office of Management and Budget, and many other agency heads whose understanding and assistance was invaluable) and to the Congress, some of whose members and staff played key roles in restoring order in a chaotic period.

As the hours of congressional hearings lengthened and the days of special meetings with environmental representatives dragged on, the reassuring images of American scientists responsibly assuming unfamiliar public service roles gradually became the expression of the dominant morality in the whole affair. Never have the intrinsic values been so visible or victorious as in this real-time test under the alert gaze of society.

In May 1989, a recombinant gene was introduced into the body of a cancer patient, permitting a new form of therapy to be monitored. Approval for this new form of therapy required many months of deliberations and turmoil including threatened injunctions. The successful outcome can be credited to the lineal descendant of the first Recombinant Advisory Committee, which saw the question through to public satisfaction. This is a victory for humankind, a further vindication of diligence and careful process in the defense of scientific values.

It is now more than a decade since I tacked the following moral onto a review of the early history of this period:

> It is possible that the "recombinant DNA affair" will someday be regarded as a social aberration, with the Guidelines preserved under glass. Even so, we can say the beginnings were honorable. Faced with real questions of theoretical risks, the scientists paused and then decided to proceed with caution. That decision gave rise to dangerous overreaction and exploitation, which gravely obstructed the subsequent course. Uncertainty of risk, however, is a compelling reason for caution. It will occur in some other areas of scientific research, and the initial response must be the same. After that, the lessons learned here should help us through the turbulence that is sure to come.[33]

FURTHER TESTS OF VALUES

Cases of alleged scientific fraud appeared as this epic battle was in progress. NIH was not prepared for its encounters with this challenge in the 1970s. The resources for investigation were minimal. I remember vividly the anger of a secretary of HEW when I explained how reluctant we were to separate a particular scientist from the means to pursue his profession, how we considered that careless bookkeeping or experimental errors should not be grounds for severance. Soon, after another, more egregious misdeed had come to light, I was directly threatened with having my delegations to award grants withdrawn if the offender were not debarred. When I replied that there were no provisions for debarment in the NIH authority, the secretary saw to the correction of this deficiency. When I appeared with the president of the National Academy of Sciences in early congressional hearings dealing with this subject, we both declared with conviction that outright scientific fraud was a rarity, although likely to occur from time to time, and that the system contained its own correctives. I believe this is certainly true with respect to the integrity of the intrinsic scientific values and the harshness of its code. Anyone found deliberately abusing the privileges of doing scientific research is rarely allowed a second chance. Fraud, however, is also a violation of clear-cut extrinsic values. A theft or grave misuse of property belonging to the public-private partnership is a crime, and investigators serving fiduciary agencies must do their duty.

I doubt that current efforts to give scientific fraud more definition will be helpful, or that the bookkeeping of scientists will bear statutory prescription. I think the suggested creation of new offices of standards of scientific conduct is the least desirable, if these auditors are to be suspended in a layer of government removed from intimate understanding of the intrinsic values of science and deprived of institutional memory.

At the same time, I think it is entirely possible that the intrinsic values may not be up to entrepreneurial tests of the times. In several cases of obvious fraud, legitimate questions have been raised about how seriously coauthors or preceptors have taken their responsibilities for what appears in the scientific literature. There have been deep concerns expressed about the possibility of subtle purchase of objectivity in clinical trials.[34] The perception of conflict of interest is a dark shadow over the relationship between physician and patient.

PROCESS IS ALSO A VALUE

This essay was not written to provide any personal prescription for new values necessary for medical science to maintain its purpose of serving humanity. Rather the intent has been an exercise in descriptive ethics, showing examples of how cultural values are continually being aligned with the intrinsic values of scientific inquiry in the public-private partnership which exists in academic medical science in this country. The task has never been easy. The scientists work mainly in far-flung institutions traditionally unorganized to reach consensus on scientific values, and there is, naturally, resistance to change. The public reactions, as translated mainly through the Congress, are highly pluralistic and not always informed. Processes have been developed, however, for serving the interests of scientists and public alike. Examples are to be found in the history of the NIH, for half a century the principal steward of government-financed biomedical and behavioral research. Better processes themselves have been part of the newer values emerging from this experience.

These examples have helped prove that scientific research works best when it is a self-regulating process. When we scientists fail to prove that this is so, we risk reactions that may imperil both public and science. Without exception, the best interests of each lie in the direction of unstinting search for knowledge and understanding.

NOTES

1. A. McGehee Harvey, *The Association of American Physicians 1886–1986* (Baltimore: Waverly Press, 1986), p. 191.
2. James Howard Means, *The Association of American Physicians, Its First Seventy-five Years* (New York: McGraw-Hill, 1961), p. 248.
3. Norman Howard Jones, "Human Experimentation in Historical and Ethical Perspectives," *Social Science Medicine* 16 (1982): 1429–1448.
4. William A. Yaremchuk, "The Cancer War: The Movement to Establish the National Cancer Institute, 1927–1937" (Ph.D. diss., New York University, 1977).
5. Victoria A. Harden, *Inventing the NIH: Federal Biomedical Research Policy, 1887–1937* (Baltimore: Johns Hopkins University Press, 1986).
6. Donald C. Swain, "The Rise of a Research Empire: NIH, 1930–1950," *Science* 138 (1962): 1233–1237.
7. Irwin Stewart, *Organizing Scientific Research for War* (Boston: Little, Brown, 1948); A. Hunter Dupree, "The Great Instauration of 1940: The Organization of Scientific Research for War," in *The Twentieth Century Sciences*, ed. Gerald Holton (New York: W. W. Norton, 1970); Stephen P.

Strickland, *Politics, Science and Dread Disease* (Cambridge, Mass.: Harvard University Press, 1972); Daniel M. Fox, "The Politics of the NIH Extramural Program, 1937–1950," *Journal of History of Medicine and Applied Science* 42 (1987): 447–466; Stephen P. Strickland, *The Story of the NIH Grants Program* (New York: University Press of America, 1989).

8. Strickland, *The Story of the NIH Grants Program*, p. 18.

9. Bess Furman, *A Profile of the United States Public Health Service 1798–1948* (Washington, D.C.: Department of Health, Education, and Welfare, National Institutes of Health, 1973), p. 397.

10. Wilton R. Earle to Wyndham Miles, May 7, 1964, Wilson File, NIH Historian's Office Papers, History of Medicine Division, National Library of Medicine, Bethesda, Md. (hereinafter cited HMD/NLM).

11. Thomas Parran, "Proposed Ten-Year Postwar Program for the United States Public Health Service, November 1, 1944," MSC 202, HMD/NLM.

12. Deputy Surgeon General Crabtree in records of the Office of Management and Budget, Federal Board of Hospitalization, Bethesda Site Files, Site File Series, National Archives.

13. Comment of Dr. Frank Horsfall to Cecile Hillyer as reported in Hillyer's memorandum to Dr. Jack Masur entitled "Observation Visit to the Hospital of the Rockefeller Institute for Medical Research, New York City, May 5, 1950," NIH Central Files, B & G 250.

14. Robert K. Merton, adapted by J. Z. Moss, "Basic Research and Its Potential of Relevance," *Mount Sinai Journal of Medicine* 52 (1985): 679–684.

15. Don K. Price, "Endless Frontier or Bureaucratic Morass?" *Daedalus* 107 (Spring 1978): 75–92, issued as *The Proceedings of the American Academy of Arts and Science*.

16. C. J. Van Slyke, "New Horizons in Medical Research," *Science* 104 (1946): 561.

17. R. E. Dyer, interview with Harlan Phillips, November 13, 1963, transcript in the George Rosen Collection of Oral History Transcripts, MS C 203, HMD/NLM.

18. Strickland, *Politics, Science and Dread Disease*, p. 174.

19. See the minutes of the National Advisory Cancer Council .007, especially those of the thirty-first meeting on June 14, 1946, National Archives; also Norman Topping, interview with Bess Furman Armstrong, May 1964, notes in the Bess Furman Armstrong Papers, MSC 203, Box 21, HMD/NLM; and Resolution Adopted by the Federal Board of Hospitalization, dated Washington, D.C., November 4, 1947, Records of the Office of Management and Budget, Federal Board of Hospitalization, General Record 19 Series, National Archives.

20. Records of the National Science Foundation's Special Committee on Medical Research, 1948–1975, HMD/NLM.

21. Minutes of Meeting of the Medical Board, NIH Clinical Center, December 22, 1953, Files, Office for Protection from Research Risks, NIH, Bethesda, Md.
22. David J. Rothman, "Ethics and Human Experimentation: Henry Beecher Revisited," *New England Journal of Medicine* 317 (1987): 1195–1199.
23. Memorandum dated November 4, 1964, from Robert B. Livingston, Associate Chief for Program Development, DRFR, to Director, NIH, captioned "Progress Report on Survey of Moral and Ethical Aspects of Clinical Investigation," Files, Office for Protection from Research Risks, NIH, Bethesda, Md.
24. Interview with David Price, cited by Strickland, *The Story of the NIH Grants Program*, p. 30.
25. The ad hoc committee included Drs. Nathaniel Berlin, clinical director of the National Cancer Institute, chair; Jack Masur, director of the Clinical Center; Maitland Baldwin, clinical director of the National Institute of Neurological Diseases and Blindness; and Donald Fredrickson, clinical director of the National Heart Institute.
26. PPO 129, Policy, February 8, 1966, U.S. Public Health Service, Division of Research Grants. Memorandum dated December 12, 1966, from Surgeon General, U.S. Public Health Service, to Heads of Institutions Receiving Public Health Service Grants, captioned "Clarification of Procedure on Clinical Research and Investigation Involving Human Subjects," Files, Office for Protection from Research Risks, NIH, Bethesda, Md.
27. Henry E. Beecher, "Ethics and Clinical Research," *New England Journal of Medicine* 274 (1966): 1354–1360.
28. "The Final Report of the Tuskegee Study Ad Hoc Advisory Panel," HEW, April 28, 1973; James H. Jones, *Bad Blood: The Tuskegee Syphilis Experiment* (New York: Free Press, 1981).
29. Department of Health, Education, and Welfare, "Protection of Human Subjects," *Federal Register* 39, no. 105 (May 1974).
30. I am indebted to Dr. Charles R. McCarthy, director of the Office for Protection from Research Risks, NIH, for firsthand descriptions of these events.
31. Department of Health and Human Welfare, "Protection of Human Subjects, Fetuses, Pregnant Women, and In Vitro Fertilization," *Federal Register* 40, no. 154 (August 1975).
32. Opening of House Resolution 131, introduced by Richard Ottinger (Dem., N.Y.), January 18, 1977; Letter to Director, NIH, from Dr. Charles Yanofsky, Herzstein Professor of Biology, Stanford University, July 21, 1977.

33. Donald S. Fredrickson, "A History of the Recombinant DNA Guidelines in the United States," in *Recombinant DNA and Genetic Experimentation*, ed. Joan Morgan and W. J. Whelan (New York: Pergamon Press, 1979).

34. B. Healey, L. Campeau, R. Gray, et al., "Conflict of Interest Guidelines for a Multicenter Clinical Trial of Treatment after Coronary Artery Bypass-Graft Surgery," *New England Journal of Medicine* 320 (1989): 949–951; A. S. Relman, "Economic Incentives in Clinical Investigation," *New England Journal of Medicine* 320 (1989): 933–934.

KIM DUNN AND RUTH ELLEN BULGER

VALUES IN TEACHING AND LEARNING:

A STUDENT-TEACHER DIALOGUE

Since teaching and learning are such closely related interdependent activities, Kim Dunn and Ruth Bulger (former student and faculty member at the University of Texas Health Science Center–Houston) present their views in a dialogue. In turn they consider the factors they brought to the learning relationship, their views on the roles of students and faculty, and what they see as the ethical responsibilities in the teaching-learning perspective.

OBLIGATIONS IN LEARNING:
THE PERSPECTIVE OF A STUDENT

Teaching and learning are to education as yin and yang are to qi (life force), for their very nature involves both interaction and symbiosis. As one teaches, the other learns; and in the process of learning, the other teaches. From my perspective, the key responsibility for education rests with the student. Additional duties arise from this: to know the purpose of one's education; to know how one learns best, whether in small groups, visually, or experientially; to find mentors; to be open to new ideas; to think critically; to challenge assumptions before accepting knowledge as truth; to evaluate one's own learning and performance while working to achieve personal educational objectives; to recognize one's individual strengths and weaknesses; to be comfortable with that which is not known.

If a student has the privilege of participating in patient care, additional responsibilities are involved: to be a patient's advocate first, a learner second; to challenge the ethical conduct of others involved in the care of the patient if it is not conducive to good patient care; to be a teacher to the patient; to uphold the ethical conduct of one's chosen profession.

I was encouraged as a college student to organize my studies around educational topics and issues. I was taught to approach the faculty as advanced students of a problem or discipline. My college experience was interactive. Throughout I was reminded of and guided by the often repeated comment of my high school chemistry/ physics teacher, "I wish I could tear down the mental walls surrounding each discipline in order to help the student learn."

Upon arriving at medical school with these notions of self-guided education, I, like most of my colleagues, was in shock. We had come excited to learn how to take care of patients and the first four months were spent memorizing the biochemical cycles and dissecting a dead person. Little guidance was given about the importance of these experiences to patient care, and we had precious little time, given our work load, to seek answers from the clinical faculty.

Many medical students have made similar observations about the educational system. Having had the privilege to work with students from all U.S. medical schools for the past five years in trying to understand medical education—its process, content, and evaluation—I have learned that there is an epidemic in medical education. We have come to agree with August Swanson that the "curriculum is faculty-centered,"[1] and with Ruel Stallones that "classes and other formal didactic exercises are seen as ends in themselves and not adjuncts to learning. In too many institutions, curricula have developed into prescribed sets of courses and the purpose of the curriculum is to complete the courses. This academic dog chases his own tail around in a circle and ascribes meaning to and finds happiness in the activity."[2]

ROLES OF THE UNIVERSITY: A FACULTY PERSPECTIVE

We agree that learning is the responsibility of the student. But the faculty should play an important role in facilitating this process. What then are the fundamental ethical principles which need to be considered in a discussion of teaching from the faculty perspective?

And how are these principles relevant to the student/faculty interactions that occur?

The first universities appearing in the eleventh and twelfth centuries in England, France, Italy, and Germany started as groups of professors and their students and, of special interest to us, these universities early on included professions such as medicine, law, and theology. Therefore, the health sciences are not recent additions to our universities. The development of the American universities in the nineteenth century was affected by the unity of research and teaching found in the German universities but, in an egalitarian society such as ours, a greater diversity of educational institutions was inevitably found. However, the dual functions of research and teaching within universities were also established early.

The role of the government in funding science research was developed during the Second World War and immediately following it. Vannevar Bush, in *Science, the Endless Frontier*, established what essentially has been the national science policy since that time.[3] The science community, by its research, provides social benefits to society in return for which the government provides much of the money for the research with a large degree of independence allowed to the scientific community. The high cost of modern research technology now has made the attainment of research funding an indispensable part of academic life at research intensive institutions.

The inclusion of the teaching hospitals with their service functions into the universities provided a health care site for the medical faculty. As Steven Muller puts it, "What is unique is that medicine is the only academic discipline that incorporates so directly into its own operations, and thereby into the university itself, a large component of the industry for which it trains people."[4]

The recent proliferation of collaborative arrangements between the university and industry or government has extended the role of the university to include the translation of research findings into patient-related products. The passage of the Stevenson-Wydler Act in 1980 (PL 96-480), the Small Business Patent Procedure Act (PL 96-517) in the same year, the Economic Recovery Tax Act of 1981, and the Federal Technology Transfer Act (PL 99-502) and subsequent Executive Order 12591 have made such collaborations between industry, universities, and government a major part of the national agenda. We, as scientists, are now part of the system for facilitating technology transfer and furthering economic competitiveness. How this new role in the economic health of our country will affect the traditional values of the university is not yet clear. Issues such as the free exchange of information within the university, the choice of research projects to be undertaken by faculty, the use of public funds invested for private gain, and the effect of industrial collaboration on graduate student education have not been well investigated at this time.

The health science centers are then left with the roles of education, research, patient care, services of various kinds, as well as functions relating to technology transfer and economic competitiveness. Other pressures are weighing on faculty at the present time as well. Funds for research may become tighter in these years of fiscal deficits especially in light of problems with our aging and outmoded scientific infrastructure, which would be extremely expensive to update. Many believe that our training of scientific personnel has been slighted in recent years due to the policy of stabilization of the number of research grant awards. These personnel deficits are especially pronounced in the areas of clinical investigation and outcomes assessment research and this also needs to be addressed. The changes on the health care scene with Diagnosis Related Groups and managed care, the challenge of health care for individuals suffering from AIDS, and the increasing problems associated with the skyrocketing numbers of individuals involved with substance abuse loom large on the horizon.

The public seems angry at the rising costs of health care, and they expect to be cured with a hundred percent certainty at no risk. Some see scientists as dishonest in research, causing animals to suffer in useless experiments and giving the wrong medicine to children.

PROCESS/CONTENT/EVALUATION IN MEDICAL EDUCATION: A STUDENT'S VIEW

I understand and appreciate the diversity of roles the faculty is expected to play. However, I would like to stress the aspects of medical education that are important in developing the student's competence in confronting societal problems. Therefore, I would like to present my view of how the educational process, content, and evaluation of medical students, at least, do not prepare the students optimally for the challenges just outlined.

Process

Two different learning processes are required of students in the traditional system. For the first two years, they sit in large lecture halls for thirty to forty hours a week and listen passively. The teacher is viewed as the giver of knowledge and the student as the recipient.

During the clinical phase of training, the students are expected to remember the basic science information as the switch is made to an active, patient-oriented learning process for the next two years. This experience brings home to most students the critical need for more interaction between basic science and clinical faculty. During this phase and including residency, sleep deprivation takes its toll not only on the student and resident but also on patients by detracting from at least the noncognitive dimensions of patient care.

I think the action that is being taken in New York and California to regulate the hours and supervision of house staff should serve as a stiff warning that society is willing to begin telling academic medicine how to go about its business. Unless we begin to evaluate ourselves seriously and take corrective action, it will be done for us.

Content

What is the basic fund of knowledge? Biological scientists have their notions; public health/prevention specialists have theirs; clinicians of various fields have theirs. As experiences vary, so do points of view. I know that the information taught is important but I find that the lecture format leads to many pedagogical inadequacies. Information is ordered around discipline cues which are not usually given in the clinical context, making the information seem remote and certainly very difficult to recall two to three years later.

Students' perceptions of the adequacy of curriculum content in areas which are important for the future practice of medicine are detailed in table 1. These data, selected from the Association of American Medical Colleges graduation questionnaire,[5] show that little change occurred in students' perceptions between 1981 and 1987. Inasmuch as we do not have enough faculty bridging medicine and

Table 1. Selected Results from AAMC Graduation Questionnaire All Schools Summary, Attitude toward Amount of Instruction

Area	1981		1987	
	Excessive	Inadequate	Excessive	Inadequate
Preventive care	1.4	63.2	1.6	60.4
Public health and community medicine	5.2	50.4	3.8	51.9
Nutrition	1.2	63.9	1.3	65.7
Medical care cost control	1.2	65.1	1.5	60.3
Care of ambulatory patients	1.0	36.6	1.6	38.1
Therapeutic management	1.1	26.6	1.2	24.8
Management of patients' problems	4.0	47.3	4.0	47.9
Clinical pharmacology	2.1	25.8	2.0	31.1
Patient follow-up	0.6	47.1	0.8	47.0
Research techniques	5.4	47.9	3.9	58.2
Basic science information	17.4	8.3	24.0	5.0
Number of respondents	10,795		11,307	

public health or enough communication between the two disciplines, medical students receive information relating to prevention and health promotion only in a few lectures scheduled in late afternoon or in student-generated courses.

The observations of curricular inadequacy which I find particularly alarming are those in the areas of clinical pharmacology, research techniques, public health, and nutrition. In the area of clinical pharmacology, we have gone from a quarter to a third of graduating students feeling inadequately prepared in one of the basic means of treatment; in research techniques, it is necessary for students to have at least a rudimentary ability to think about new scientific developments and to judge competently the merits of a published clinical trial yet 58.2 percent feel inadequately prepared; with regard to public health, fundamental concepts are not stressed according to 51.9 percent of the students who responded; and for nutrition, 65.7 percent of the students feel they are ill prepared in the rudiments of nutrition, such as being able to provide advice on the latest fad diet or on what supplements to take or when and how to refer a patient to a dietician.

Evaluation

By far the favorite means of evaluation in medical education is the standardized board exam. Although I recognize the need for evaluation, the tenacity with which this form of examination is sustained reminds me of Samuel Johnson's description of a prejudiced man as "one who resolves to regulate his time by a certain watch, but will not enquire whether the watch is right or not."[6] Many students have reservations about the standard board examination approach. First, it is not often that patients arrive in the office with multiple choice questions tattooed on their chests. This form of evaluation encourages memorization and not concept formation. Second, it does not hold up well when measured by the epidemiologic concepts of internal and external validity. For a test to be internally consistent, it must evaluate students' fund of knowledge with the same questions, but we know that between years, the examination changes. With regard to external validity, one must query how this test evaluates the clinical competence of individuals.

It would seem, therefore, that evaluation of clinical performance should be more important. However, I am very disturbed by the large numbers of graduating seniors who tell me that they have never had an attending physician observe them doing a full history and physical examination or have had only one inspection, usually dur-

ing an Introduction to Clinical Medicine course. The highest percentage of graduating seniors who report that they have not had any
clinical faculty watch them perform a history and physical is 84 percent.[7] This was from a survey with a 50 percent response rate. Assuming a reporting bias such that those who turned in the survey
were only those who had not been evaluated, that still leaves a corrected percentage of 42 percent of graduating seniors who had not
been evaluated by a medical school faculty member. That is deplor-
able and unfortunately is representative of most schools. To my
knowledge, at present, the only schools having a comprehensive
evaluation of the clinical performance of students are those in
Illinois.

One hears from many students that they have worked with others
who were not team players and seized every opportunity for sliding
away from clinical duties to study for the boards. There is also the
claim that students can deliver marginal performances on the wards
but do exceptionally well on the boards and then receive a grade of
honors for the rotation. There is little honor in this. Therefore,
should we not also incorporate a peer evaluation mechanism into
the overall evaluation of students? This could also help to inculcate
the value of peer review so necessary for sustaining a profession.

But as with all epidemics, there are some very creative and committed individuals trying to improve the situation. We should be encouraged by such reports as the General Professional Education of
the Physician and the trend of problem-based learning. At present
there are several schools (Rush, New Mexico, Bowman Gray, Harvard, Southern Illinois) experimenting with this alternative method
of education. Though not a panacea, it does represent a willingness
to attempt new strategies for improving the medical education process, content, and evaluation. Some have viewed these attempts
with skepticism. However, I think that nonconformity does not imply a lowering of standards; it can be, as I believe it is in the case of
problem-based learning, an instrument of progress, based upon a rational interpretation of the present and future needs of physicians in
clinical practice.

I am also encouraged by many of the AAMC's efforts to facilitate the improvement of medical education for its constituent medical schools: clinical evaluation workshops, problem-based learning

workshops, the Assessing Change in Medical Education project, which promises to be the modern equivalent of the Flexner report, the establishment of a division of minority health promotion in the AAMC, the renewed vigor for incorporating student input into the Liaison Committee on Medical Education review process, and the new movement to evaluate the hours and supervision issues of house staff. The national boards are being revised to improve on the clinical component and the possibility of establishing a pass/fail evaluation mechanism is under consideration.

In essence, it is the students' responsibility to become educated and competent by drawing from the environment that which is useful and by supplementing this information and experience through their own efforts when answers are lacking. However, a nurturing environment is helpful if not necessary. I think a truthful ranking of the stated goals of an academic institution regarding research, teaching, and service would reveal that education is valued the least. One of the overriding unwritten goals of institutions is to achieve some level of prestige in the eyes of the academic community, not necessarily the local community. This objective tends to orient an institution's efforts toward research discoveries and contributions to medical care technology, because these increase its status in the national academic community. The trend to ignore teaching in favor of research is exacerbated by our current inability to measure educational contributions and by the fact that education brings in little money.

E. F. Schumacher, in *Small Is Beautiful: Economics As If People Mattered*, defines the value of education: "All history—as well as all current experience—points to the fact that it is man, not nature, who provides the primary resource: that the key factor of all economic development comes out of the mind of man. Suddenly, there is an outburst of daring, initiative, invention, constructive activity, not in one field alone, but in many fields all at once. No one may be able to say where it came from in the first place; but we can see how it maintains and even strengthens itself: through various kinds of schools, in other words, through education. In a very real sense, therefore, we can say that education is the most vital of all resources."[8] Why, then, is it so difficult for an academic health center to value education?

ETHICS OF EDUCATION: A FACULTY PERSPECTIVE

I agree that there are deficiencies in various dimensions of medical education as it is presently being undertaken that could be corrected. Perhaps it would be useful to look at the views of some people concerning ethical aspects of the educational process.

Lord Eric Ashby, in a lecture in 1969, asserted that inherent in the discipline of scholarship is a set of ethical values which includes a reverence for truth incorporating the recognition that all truth may be contaminated by error; an appreciation of equality, because any scholar who advances knowledge has a place; and a recognition of internationalism, for the pursuit and acquisition of new knowledge do not recognize national borders and one's theories can be upset by persons from any culture.[9]

Edward Shils, in his book *The Academic Ethic*, says that the primary role of the university is not only the methodical discovery of truths but the transmission of these truths to students, the enhancement of the students' understanding of them, and the training of students in the attitudes and critical methodology necessary to make new discoveries as free from error as possible. Reassessment and revision are also essential since new discoveries and insights make frequent reevaluation necessary.[10]

The health sciences university not only shares these types of educational responsibilities but has added ones as well. It must instruct its students in many technical procedures while participating in the process of health care delivery in the teaching setting. Due to the importance of preventive medicine, it also needs to play a role in the education of society itself.

One feature that distinguishes a profession is its members' reflection on the ethical traditions which govern it. If teaching can be classified as a profession, what then are the ethical traditions to which members of this profession might adhere?

Shils has undertaken a broad analysis of the ethics of education and stresses the following obligations that faculty have to their students:

1. The faculty should aim at conveying an understanding of the fundamental truths of a subject and of the methods of inquiry used to obtain them.

2.   During the process of conveying material, the faculty should avoid making political or ethical statements which appear to be scientific or scholarly statements.

3.   It is imperative to avoid discrimination among students on the basis of the students' political or ethical ideals (it goes without saying that discrimination on the basis of gender, religion, or ethnic or social origin is absolutely antithetical to the academic ethic).

4.   Faculty must teach what is true and important without falling into dogmatism in the exposition of the subject.

5.   An openness to students' questions about the validity of propositions being put forth is required.

6.   The student should be treated with seriousness and respect and assessed fairly.

7.   Equality of opportunity is required.

8.   The faculty must not use their positions of power to have any negative impact on the students' future.

9.   They must avoid sexual relationships with students or any other means of exploitation of their authority.

Derek Bok extends these obligations to include preparing students to engage in the continuing acquisition of knowledge and understanding, as well as learning methods of intellectual inquiry and discourse. He makes a leap here and says that with the continuing presence of a formidable array of national problems, one should teach perspectives and methods for exploring large questions and imbue undergraduates with a sense of commitment and civic concern that will cause them to devote themselves to these problems. An increase in mid-career education is therefore also important.

In further relating health science teaching to its ethical foundation, I would like to expand the following aspects for consideration: the requirement for scholarly competence in one's discipline, the ability to communicate information effectively in order to facilitate learning, the need to treat students with justice and caring, the obligation to stimulate creativity, and the requirement not to exercise undue control over the student's actions and thoughts.

Competence and Communication

A teacher of modern science at a graduate level must maintain scholarly competence. Harm can occur if the teacher provides incorrect information to the student. The teacher should guide the students to accurately identify what is known, and distinguish it from what is unknown or poorly understood. The teacher should be cognizant of general educational issues. Many individuals have stressed the pedagogical importance of concentrating on central intellectual principles and not on excessive amounts of detailed information.[11]

One of the general educational issues in recent years has been an interest in the use of noncognitive criteria in the evaluation of medical students since these criteria can serve as tools for professionalization and as stimuli for administrative action. Grant Miller et al. surveyed 135 medical schools to see if they used noncognitive criteria in evaluation of students. Of the eighty-eight schools that returned the questionnaires, 54.5 percent indicated that they possessed written noncognitive criteria. Among the thirty-one sets of noncognitive criteria, the expectations mentioned most frequently were honesty (81 percent), professional behavior (77 percent), dedication to learning (62 percent), appearance (42 percent), respect for law (42 percent), respect for others (42 percent), confidentiality (35 percent), substance abuse (19 percent), and financial responsibility (19 percent).[12]

Bok maintains that having an environment that rewards good teaching is a basic step in improving our educational institutions.[13] Many professional schools do not have highly developed abilities to assess fairly and effectively the instructional performance of individual faculty. David Irby at the University of Washington has done a great deal to provide objective ways to evaluate teaching.[14] He summarizes those factors in addition to disciplinary competence which facilitate learning:

1. Organization of material
2. Clarity of presentation
3. The ability to listen and entertain questions openly
4. The ability to establish goals and effectively evaluate progress
5. Transmission of a sense of wonder and curiosity

Justice and Caring

Another area which should be of ethical concern is that of interpersonal relationships. Lawrence Kohlberg stresses the constitutional guarantee of each individual's right to justice.[15] Central to the theory of justice are equity, equality, and liberty. The teacher must assure equal access to materials, instruction, and remediation as well as equitable standards for evaluation.

Carol Gilligan, in her excellent book entitled *In a Different Voice*, discerns a different path to moral development from the one described by Kohlberg, that of the ethics of care. In this concept, moral development is evidenced by mutual caring and responsible relationships which allow one to act responsibly toward both self and others and thereby to sustain connection. Just how this mutual caring should be expressed in a faculty/student relationship would vary depending on the situation, the environment, and the personalities of the faculty member and the student involved.

Gilligan then combines her theory with Kohlberg's into an "ethics of justice and care, the ideal human relationship—the vision that self and other will be treated as of equal worth, that despite differences in power, things will be fair; the vision that everyone will be responded to and included, that no one will be left alone or hurt." [16] To me this describes a faculty-student relationship characterized by a reinforcement of the worth and dignity of each of the parties in a mutual, honest, and voluntary way. It must respect both students' and faculty members' needs and thereby be conducive to stimulation of both teaching and learning.

The increasing literature on medical student stress reviewed by Strayhorn indicates that much can be wrong within medical education. The stresses which students identify include areas such as the methods of instruction and evaluation, the overload of information that students perceive as having little relevance, competition among peers, inadequate communication between students and faculty, patient encounters when students lack adequate skills, and time demands that delay emotional and social development.

Creativity

One role of teaching should be to encourage originals. Originality and creative potential are necessary for the discovery of new medical knowledge. Silvano Arieti, in his book *Creativity: The Magic Synthesis*, discusses social factors which facilitate creativity. [17] Among these factors are:

1. An openness to cultural stimuli
2. Stress on becoming (growth), not just on being (the fleeting moment)
3. Free access to cultural media for all citizens without discrimination
4. Exposure to different or even contrasting cultural stimuli
5. Tolerance for and an interest in divergent views
6. The promotion of incentives and awards
7. Freedom after repression
8. The interaction of significant persons

Freedom from Undue Control

History has made it evident that when people are part of institutions in which they are dependent on the actions of superiors, moral wrongs can occur. M. Scott Peck, in looking for a medical diagnosis of evil, cautions against the use of power to destroy the spiritual growth of others for selfish purposes.[18] Erving Goffman identifies problems by analyzing behavior within closed institutions such as asylums and prisons, and Robert Lifton, in his study of Nazi doctors, cautions against psychic numbing (the general category of the diminished capacity to feel).[19] They all probe the underlying dynamics of institutions which somehow could explain the abuse of power leading to the limitations on rights of the individuals in the group. Instances of infractions of personal freedom, such as sexual harassment, continue to occur even in our best institutions. Since faculty can affect the careers of their students, they need to continually examine their motives with respect to individual students and the intellectual property of the students.

Much of what has been discussed so far relates to general principles of education. What special considerations does the environment for teaching in a health science center place on the faculty?

The Basic Science Years

Faculty members in the basic medical sciences have been well educated in the area of their scientific investigations. They generally have received little information on educational principles. Ph.D.

faculty members who teach much of the first two years in a traditional curriculum have had little or no experience with the content
of clinical disciplines which might help them stress material particularly relevant to clinical decision making. In discussing the standard four-year medical school curriculum, August Swanson says,
"Their [the faculty's] comfort, in significant measure, is derived from
its almost immutable constancy. Its lack of demand for intellectual
rigor in educational planning and its easy accommodation to faculty
members' research and service responsibilities have frozen this medical education model in place. It allows faculties to believe that they
are fulfilling their educational responsibilities while making the
least demand on them. It is no wonder that students perceive that
they are lowest on the totem pole of faculty priorities. Medical
education in the United States is faculty centered not student centered."[20] The Association of American Medical Colleges' report on
physicians for the twenty-first century stresses a curriculum revision
which encourages the development of skills, values, and attitudes by
students while limiting the amount of material that they are expected to commit to memory.[21]

Teaching in the Clinical Arena

Much of the student's education in the clinical years takes place in
the patient care arena. In this area, physicians have long included
the use of codes and oaths of no legal but of considerable moral
significance to express their covenantal relationship with patients
and their commitment to the education of future health care providers. Medical leadership has provided much definition of what
constitutes ethical behavior in clinical medicine and much self-
regulation in the processes of teaching, certification, and accreditation. Although state governments license physicians, generally most
of the process is controlled by physicians. The rise in use of modern
technology in patient care has thrust many new ethical dilemmas to
the fore in clinical medicine. In spite of the new emphasis on these
ethical dilemmas, there is still some dissatisfaction with the lack of
meaningful human interaction resulting from shortened hospital
stays and the use of advanced technology for diagnosis and treatment in lieu of a thorough history and physical.

Teaching of Graduate Students in Various Research Settings

Graduate education is a more active kind of learning than medical education in which students work closely with faculty to learn how to pose questions, design ways to test their hypotheses, and execute experiments (often with the aid of other faculty who have devised new methods useful in testing hypotheses). However, there remain other educational issues in graduate student education which faculty must handle, such as how best to instruct students in the responsible conduct of their research, how to provide the most humane use of experimental animals in research, and how to protect students from any compromising of their educational experiences which could arise from their mentor's collaboration with industry.

A NEW ENVIRONMENT FOR THE FUTURE: A STUDENT'S VIEW

I agree that there are different approaches to education in various areas of the health sciences. I recently attended two graduation ceremonies at the University of Texas Health Science Center at Houston, one for the School of Public Health and the other for the Graduate School of Biomedical Sciences, both of which were held in the same auditorium some eighteen hours apart. During the graduation exercise, the students at the School of Public Health were reminded of the many public health issues before them today such as environmental crises, drug abuse, violence, and AIDS. The students at the Graduate School of Biomedical Sciences were reminded of the explosive future of the "new biology." At neither ceremony did speakers mention issues facing graduates in the other field. However, both groups of graduates were encouraged to value teaching as an honor. I was reminded of the need for "bridge people"—bridging patient care and laboratory science, patient care and public health, and public health and laboratory science. While watching the students leave the stage with diplomas in hand, I realized that there promises to be a different environment for the next generation of faculty and students of health science centers.

In no area do I sense the urgency for a bridging of health science disciplines more than in the gap between public health and medicine. I feel that both are fast losing the ethic of care—physicians for individuals and public health for populations. Physicians have been soundly criticized for the emphasis on remuneration, lack of apparent concern for the patient, and lack of time given to individual patients. Epidemiology, the basic science of preventive medicine, has been consumed for the past thirty years with developing new ways of thinking about methodology and wanting to be accepted as a "real science."[22] What is of even more concern is the misunderstanding and therefore basic mistrust which divide public health and medicine. At the national level, the AAMC and organized public health do little talking. At the local level, there is a very small number of joint appointments between medical schools and schools of public health and neither of the medical schools in Houston has a formal M.D./M.P.H. program with the School of Public Health. One way to regain the ethic of care is to work jointly to assess the needs of the community in which a medical and a public health institution co-exist and to develop creative ways in which care for vulnerable and indigent individuals of the community can be given. For example, the Texas Medical Center is one of the most complex academic health environments, yet it is part of a community in which the infant mortality rate in certain populations rivals that of many third world countries. Is this mortality rate to be viewed as a social problem which therefore does not fall under the purview of an academic medical center? Or, should this not instead be viewed by the academic medical center as a preventable cause of very early mortality?

The moral imperative aside, we simply can no longer afford the luxury of isolation. For example, the growing emphasis on health services research as a viable academic discipline demands cooperation. Patient care is not often done at a school of public health and expertise in research design and evaluation is not always found in schools of medicine; and yet we need to combine patients, clinicians, and epidemiologists in order to produce high-quality health services research. The two faculties should work jointly to answer the question of what basic level of health care is required for a given problem.

As a service to the community at large, academic medicine has an opportunity to provide leadership in defining the questions for society in this area—not the responsibility for decision, only for defining the issues and outlining potential solutions. If the experts in areas of research, service, and education cannot frame the questions, then who can?

ETHICAL RESPONSIBILITIES OF THE INSTITUTION AND THE INDIVIDUAL FACULTY

It is important to recognize the role of leadership in helping to build bridges across various disciplines to meet the challenge of our changing environment. In that light, I would like to consider what institutions might do to assure ethical approaches to teaching and then whether this is done or not, what the individual faculty member's obligation might be.

Institutional Mechanisms

Institutions need ways for the leadership, on both the administrative and faculty levels, to reflect upon and consciously define the values which they wish to preserve within the teaching programs of their individual institutions in the midst of the present change. The means of preserving these values may well vary from institution to institution depending upon the particular mission for which each institution is striving. Leadership in this area could come from the administration or from faculty governance committees prompted by individual faculty. Questions to be considered might relate to which educational curriculum would best encourage student learning, the stimulation of responsible conduct of research, and potential problems for graduate student education relating to the increase in industrial collaborations and to other entrepreneurial activities on the part of the teaching faculty. Further questions might address the exposure of basic science faculty to clinical problems and clinical decision making to give them greater perspective on which important concepts to stress in their teaching.

Once the values are defined, the institution can help by establishing guidelines for ethical behavior for teaching in the classrooms, in laboratories, and in clinical situations which will preserve these values.

Finally, ways must be found to reward faculty for their teaching efforts in the classroom, the laboratory, and the clinic, as well as in the community. At the present time, the system for rewards and recognition for health science teaching is such that teaching is not a high priority for faculty effort. In order for the reward system to work, there must be a way to evaluate educational efforts and that evaluation must be done in a consistent and fair manner.

There often is a lack of understanding of basic educational principles in the health center environment. Faculty can be exceptionally well prepared for their scientific endeavors but less well prepared to consider curricular issues such as alternative instructional methods or how to handle large classes of highly intelligent students in the most useful way. Graduating health professionals also need to be cognizant of educational principles to help patients learn. A variety of mechanisms can be used to accomplish this kind of enrichment of the environment, including the circulation of educational journals or articles, providing leaders knowledgeable in this area, and the introduction of useful material concerning educational principles into the graduate and health professional curricula.

The Role of the Individual Health Professional

I believe that in modern-day life, the biggest impediment to a moral life is not malevolence or evil intentions but a lack of time to reflect on our motives or actions. How often do we feel like the rabbit in *Alice in Wonderland* who lacked the time to say hello or good-bye because of lateness? This lack of time to consider our actions and words engenders a numbness to the implications of our actions.

With or without institutional guidelines, we are still responsible for our individual ethical behavior with respect to student instruction. I am struck by the words of Thomas Lickona, "Let me say, too, that ethics needs to be on the daily agenda, not reserved only for matters of great moment. Momentous moral decisions about nuclear energy, the distribution of fuel, genetic screening, and human conception in the laboratory are obviously great challenges before ethics, but they are rare events, not the stuff of our day-to-day moral lives. Whether to declare everything on our income tax when money is tight and the government wastes a lot of it, whether to conserve fuel when it is inconvenient to do so, whether to be democratic when it is easier to make the decision ourselves, whether to give someone time when our time is short, whether to object to small corruptions when silence is more expedient, whether to be decent to our subordinates and fair with our children—these are the moral choices that, taken together, determine the quality of moral life in society. There is a need to cultivate an 'ethics of the everyday,' a morality of minor affairs, that translates respect for persons into small deeds of kindness, honesty, and decency." [23]

Bok discusses the role that institutions of higher learning should be playing in the moral development of their students: "Even if presidents are overburdened and professors happen to prepare themselves in specialized disciplines, universities have an obligation to try to help their students understand how to lead ethical, reflective, fulfilling lives. One can appreciate the difficulty of the task and understand if progress is slow and halting. What is harder to forgive is a refusal to recognize the problem or to acknowledge a responsibility to work at it conscientiously." [24] In order to accomplish this, I believe that our faculties will need to consider carefully what our educational system is teaching students on this ethical level. Kenneth Keniston says, "But perhaps the place to start is with the experience of the medical student himself. For there is much evidence that we come to treat others as we have been treated ourselves. Medical students are sometimes treated as if they were merely rote learners of specialized technical competence. But in fact they are human beings—distinctively motivated young men and women who have chosen to undergo the often arduous initiation into the vocational hazards of medicine. If this fact could be more openly recognized by medical schools, and if the effort to teach competence could be supplemented with an effort to strengthen students' sensitivity and openness to themselves and others, then future physicians might be better supported in their desire to treat their patients not merely competently, but wisely, responsibly, and humanely." [25]

If a profession is distinguished by the reflection of its members on the ethical traditions which govern it and by its ability to self-regulate, this requires the faculty to take seriously their own definition of standards by which they will operate—standards not only for classroom teaching but for teaching during patient care situations, teaching in the research laboratory, and defining relationships with industry, especially as they affect the training of our graduate students.

ETHICAL RESPONSIBILITIES OF
THE STUDENT FOR CHANGE

Students also have responsibilities in this regard. They should not be afraid to provide leadership because of their low status in the power structure of an institution. There is, in fact, a liberating strength in a status which yields nothing to protect. Students do not have to worry about tenure, grants, or what a chairperson will do—none of the baggage with which faculty have to contend. There exists an ethical responsibility for students to organize and to voice concerns collectively in open and honest dialogue with faculty and administrators. If problems exist, bringing together experience and new ideas can begin to define them and thereby start on the path toward solutions. If there are strengths, these should be celebrated and built upon. Students and teachers both have the responsibility to continue this constructive dialogue within the institution, regarding the explicit and implicit values as they are expressed through the institution, so that the interplay between individual and institutional values remains dynamic and creative.

The students bring new ideas, value emphasis, and perspectives on societal needs. Rarely are these quickly incorporated into the curriculum, nor should they be. Usually innovations come through pilot programs and informal learning opportunities on such things as preventive medicine, nutrition, ethics, history of the profession, health policy, and new courses on basic medical science. Many students from various health science disciplines are taking an active role, working with faculty to develop learning opportunities for themselves and each other.

In Houston, students from the University of Texas and Baylor are working well together to encourage administrators to formalize joint M.D./Ph.D. programs, establishing a Baylor–University of Texas clinic staffed by volunteer public health, nursing, pharmacy, law, and medical students and faculty. In addition to providing primary care, the clinic provides an opportunity for pilot projects designed to determine the needs of the community served. We are attempting to get faculty from the School of Public Health and to encourage both medical schools to assist the students in understanding the needs of various vulnerable populations and taking an active role with the faculty to assist the community with demonstration projects. Finally, we will hold a conference to look at the future roles of our academic medical center in indigent care within the context of the traditional values of education, research, and service.

We feel that students from all disciplines can work together on a common problem, thus mutually enhancing their education while also making progress toward amelioration of community problems. Such joint efforts can enhance the spirit of cooperation among different health science disciplines, encouraging more collaborative effort in the future.

Finally, it shall be up to us to sustain the spirit of change as we move from the sheltered role of students into roles requiring more from us in the areas of service, research, and education. We look to our faculty and administrators as advanced students of the health sciences to share in that spirit and responsibility.

NOTES

1. August G. Swanson, "Medical Students: A Substrate and a Legacy," *Journal of Pediatrics* 112 (1988): 1023–1026.
2. Ruel A. Stallones, *New Approaches in Schools of Public Health: Present and Future*, ed. J. Z. Bowers and E. F. Purcell (New York: Independent Publishers Group, 1973).
3. Vannevar Bush, *Science, the Endless Frontier*, a Report to the President on a Program for Postwar Scientific Research, Office of Scientific Research and Development, July 1945, reprinted by the National Science Foundation, May 1980.
4. Steven Muller, "The Medical School and the University," *Journal of the American Medical Association* 252 (1984): 1455–1457.
5. Graduation questionnaire for the years 1981 and 1987, Association of American Medical Colleges, Washington, D.C.
6. James Boswell, *The Life of Samuel Johnson* (London: Charles Dilly in the Poultry Publishers, 1791).
7. Personal communication from the senior class of one of the 127 medical schools approved by the U.S. Liaison Committee on Medical Education.
8. E. F. Schumacher, *Small Is Beautiful: Economics As If People Mattered* (New York: Harper & Row, 1973).
9. Eric Ashby, *Adapting Universities to a Technological Society* (San Francisco: Jossey-Bass Publishers, 1974).
10. Edward Shils, "The Report of a Study Group of the International Coun-

cil on the Future of the University," in *The Academic Ethic* (Chicago: University of Chicago Press, 1983).

11. Derek Bok, *Higher Learning* (Cambridge, Mass.: Harvard University Press, 1986); Richard C. Mulgan, "The Role of Universities in Professional Education," *New Zealand Medical Journal* 99 (1986): 107–110; G. Strayhorn, "Effect of a Major Curriculum Revision on Students' Perceptions of Well-Being," *Academic Medicine* 64 (1989): 25–29.

12. Grant D. Miller, Daniel Frank, Ronald D. Franks, and Carl J. Getto, "Noncognitive Criteria for Assessing Students in North American Medical Schools," *Academic Medicine* 64 (1989): 42–45.

13. Bok, *Higher Learning* and "Toward Education of Quality," *Harvard Magazine* (May/June 1986).

14. David M. Irby, "Evaluating Teaching Skills," *Diabetes Educator* 11 (Supp. PPL, 1985): 37–46.

15. Lawrence Kohlberg, "Education for Justice: A Modern Statement of the Platonic View," in *Moral Education*, ed. N. F. Sizer and T. R. Sizer (Cambridge, Mass.: Harvard University Press, 1970), pp. 57–83.

16. Carol Gilligan, *In a Different Voice: Psychological Theory and Women's Development* (Cambridge, Mass.: Harvard University Press, 1982).

17. Silvano Arieti, *Creativity: The Magic Synthesis* (New York: Basic Books, 1976).

18. M. Scott Peck, *People of the Lie: The Hope for Healing Human Evil* (New York: Simon & Schuster, 1983).

19. Erving Goffman, *Asylums: Essays on the Social Situation of Mental Patients and Other Inmates* (New York: Doubleday, 1961); Robert J. Lifton, *The Nazi Doctors: Medical Killing and the Psychology of Genocide* (New York: Basic Books, 1986).

20. Swanson, "Medical Students."

21. "Physicians for the Twenty-first Century: Report of the Project Panel of the General Professional Education of the Physicians and College Preparation for Medicine," *Journal of Medical Education* 59 (1984).

22. Ruel A. Stallones, "To Advance Epidemiology," *Annual Review of Public Health* 1 (1980): 69–82.

23. Thomas Lickona, "What Does Moral Psychology Have to Say to the Teacher of Ethics?" in *Ethics Teaching in Higher Education*, ed. D. Callahan and S. Bok (New York: Plenum Press, 1980), pp. 103–132.

24. Derek Bok, "Ethics, the University, and Society," *Harvard Magazine* (May/June 1988): 39–50.

25. Kenneth Keniston, "The Medical Student," *Yale Journal of Biology and Medicine* 39 (1967): 346–358.

The Treatment of People

STANLEY JOEL REISER

HOSPITALS AS

HUMANE CORPORATIONS

In the twentieth century health care has moved inexorably away from control by individual practitioners. In their place institutions have assumed dominance. The beginning of this transition was captured by William Mayo, a founder of the clinic bearing his name, when he pronounced in 1912: "So vast is the extent of knowledge to be gained of disease that no one man can hope to accomplish more than a small share during his lifetime. The old-time practitioner has passed away, and with him has passed individualism in medicine."[1] In this period the consolidation of practice into corporate entities was led by hospitals, which rose in number from about four hundred in 1875 to over four thousand in 1909. Since then practitioners have gradually formed themselves into groups, and in very recent times many hospitals themselves have done the same.

Alteration of the structure of the health care system by this process of corporatization has significant effects on the values used within the system that underlie its decisions. Yet it is noteworthy that the modern study and reevaluation of the ethical values of health care have been focused on the relationship of person with person and have been remarkably distant from the ethical issues resulting from the actions of corporate entities in health care. This perhaps is the result of the dominant role of the individual actor in health care in its past history, where the physician or the nurse took charge and made choices. Ethical writings and discourse of the past focused on their actions, as have those of the modern period which has added another person to the small pantheon of powerful holders of rights and makers of medical decisions: the patient. Possibly this individualist focus has distracted us from recognizing the growing dominance of corporate authorities and values in health care.

THE HUMANE CORPORATION

What is most remarkable about the actions of patients seeking medical care is that they lower the defenses ordinarily used in encounters with strangers. How extraordinary the typical medical encounter is! The potential patient visits an institution to see a stranger who is a doctor (most medical encounters are with doctors who are little or not at all known to patients). The patient reveals to the stranger personal events and thoughts, disrobes, permits the body to be observed, perhaps poked, gives in to requests for the withdrawal of blood and examinations with abstruse technologies, agrees to take disagreeable medicines or, in the extreme, to allow the surgical knife to pierce the skin and explore the depths of the body to remove what the doctor/stranger thinks is necessary.

Such openness in the face of the unknown is possible for patients only because of an abiding belief that the doctor/stranger will not take advantage of the situation or, more positively, will seek the patient's welfare. The great vulnerability we carry into our encounters with medicine demands a profound commitment by those before whom this vulnerability is displayed to prove worthy of being allowed to act in its presence.

As medical actions increasingly take place in corporate settings in which participants are affected deeply by corporate rules and goals that become reified as policies, understanding corporate ethics and the ethos that creates them is essential. At the heart of this matter are the effect of the absolute growth of corporate power on the actions of medical care and the effect of a dichotomy of values within health care institutions: those underlying corporate policies and the values held and transmitted by the professional staff who work within the institution's walls.

There are in hospitals two powerful cultures whose relationship exists in tension. One is the professional culture—focused on giving care to the individual who is the patient, present-oriented because of the urgencies of illness and injury, and principally directed by values that secure patient welfare such as confidentiality and truth. The other is the corporate culture—focused on the collective needs of the patients that comprise its constituents, future-oriented through a concern for generational continuity and growth, and principally emphasizing values that insure institutional survival such as financial responsibility and duty to benefactors or shareholders.

Some of the staff within these two cultures have responsibilities that make them residents of both, others live fundamentally in one culture but are drawn by events to journey intermittently into the other, taking its perspective and embracing its values. However, on the whole the social arrangements of each group produce conformity to the norms of its principal culture.

The cultures exist in a relationship not only of tension but of symbiosis as well. The welfare of each culture depends on the success of the other, success meaning an ability to secure the values that permit the culture to function. Through the furthering of corporate values the institution is enabled to survive; through the maintenance of professional values the institution is directed to humane purpose. Ironically the triumph of one at the expense of the other leads to the demise of both: humane purpose without survival or survival without humane purpose being equally repugnant choices for the hospital.

This arrangement produces conflict not only between the cultures but also within individuals who may see the benefit of each culture's position on a given problem and become torn by the dilemma of choice. It also produces situations where the two cultures, acting from different motives, jointly endorse an action that diminishes the legitimacy of the hospital to the title of a humane corporation. The situation of joint action toward unworthy ends is as significant and pernicious for the cultures as divisive conflict between them.

There are then two fundamental aspects of institutional life in hospitals to consider: creating an environment where humane and corporate ends can be pursued harmoniously, and preventing a schism between the main cultural constituencies of the hospital. The development of hospital policy on the issues of incompetent physicians and hours of resident duty provides a view of the first problem; the approach taken to the indigent patient presents a view of the second.

THE INCOMPETENT CLINICIAN

The first section of the Hippocratic Oath, comprising more than a third of its content, discusses the relationship of physicians in training to each other and to their teachers.[2] Suffused through this passage is one dominant image—the image of family. Students were to be their teachers' children and each other's siblings in sharing the knowledge and income they would acquire. Belief by these students that the bonds of family defined the collegial relationship in medicine was crucial to assuring ethical behavior when they left the environment and scrutiny of the apprenticeship and practiced without oversight in the Greek world beyond. To foreswear the ethical duties to which one was pledged would be to dishonor not just a medical friend but a family member.

While the allegiance of physicians to each other has served historically to constrain unethical behavior, it also made difficult the honoring of one aspect of the doctor's responsibilities, stated forcefully in the 1957 Principles of Medical Ethics of the American Medical Association: "The medical profession should safeguard the public and itself against physicians deficient in moral character or professional competence. . . . They should expose, without hesitation, illegal or unethical conduct in fellow members of the profession."[3] Similar directives are found in virtually all modern codes of ethics in the health care professions. Having invoked the image of family as the defining relationship of colleague to colleague in medicine, how does one honor the injunction to expose publicly a "family" member's incompetence?

Virtually all hospitals in modern times have struggled with this problem, have been intimidated by the difficulties it raises, and usually have failed in efforts to solve it. Incidents of such failure occasionally make headlines as did a 1975 case involving twin New York City gynecologists, the Marcus brothers. These doctors, as William F. May notes, "allowed themselves to become addicted to barbiturates, to miss appointments, and to offer consultation, diagnoses, and treatment while under the observable influence of drugs. They retained skill and expertise enough, however, to refrain from killing any of their patients. Their colleagues and the institutions in which they worked were slow to blow the whistle on them."[4]

The issue has many dimensions. Most significant, perhaps, is the widely held notion that the object of identifying incompetent behavior is solely to assign blame for errors committed by the colleague in question. Instead policy should make clear that the objective is to help—to restore lost medical skill so that patients will not be endangered and professional pride can be regained. The process through which this is accomplished should be spelled out clearly in hospital procedure so that those who raise the issue do not feel their jobs are in jeopardy as a consequence—a particularly critical matter when one lower down in the hospital hierarchy queries the actions of one higher up. Those whose actions are called into question must be assured that inquiries will be conducted under a veil of confidentiality. Further, all must believe that efforts will be made, where possible, to impose restrictions only on medical skills found inadequate rather than to advocate complete exclusion from all practice. The fear that a voice raised against these physicians might cause them to be banned from practice tends to stifle the raising of that voice.

In meeting this issue, both professional and administrative staff reinforce one another and generally participate in evasive actions—the first invoking the bonds of collegial allegiance, the second protecting itself from the legal and financial discord involved in disenfranchising a person from practice that would threaten institutional growth and stability. Here, conflict between the cultures is not the problem—lack of open dialogue and commitment among them to develop an appropriate response is. On this issue, both cultures need to recognize that the ethos of the humane corporation requires action, lest the corporate body remain without the humaneness that is its soul.

RESIDENT HOURS

The hospital gives clear evidence of where its values lie in its policy for determining the hours worked by its residents. The resident has become, along with the nurse, the therapeutic mainstay of hospitals. Hospitals thus greatly benefit from gaining maximum working time from the resident. The problem of an appropriate number of hours of work is bound up in the question of what a resident is: a student who needs the long hours of learning to become an effective physician?

An employee working long hours for relatively low wages to serve the hospital? Or both? This last and conjoined view perhaps comes closest to defining the resident.

Since the resident must fulfill a certain term of work to be accepted by a specialty board as completing the requirements for certification, the resident is not at full liberty to refuse assigned duty. This constraint on the freedom of residents makes them specially vulnerable to pressure from hospitals, which derive significant patient care and financial benefit from their situation.

Central to considering this matter is the question of what the residency experience does to residents, not just to their skill with medical technology but also to their self-development and growth into mature individuals able to understand and be empathic with patients. Does the environment of residency learning mold them into humane practitioners? Or does it create callousness and cynicism?

Recently, other important considerations have been raised about the relationship between long duty hours, fatigue, and physician error, leading to legislation in New York and California restricting on-call time and total weekly resident hours. Whatever the outcome of the needed future studies on the validity of the above connections, administrators and professional staff dealing with this policy question will have an opportunity to determine what values should govern the conditions under which key learners and employees shall function in their hospitals. The humane corporation should feel strong obligations to discuss the matter openly and to make the best allocation of resources possible under the circumstances. Not just the outcome but the process under which it is determined counts greatly. Sensitivity and concern for vulnerable patients on the part of the resident staff cannot easily flourish in an environment where the same sensitivity and concern are not expressed by the hospital about the vulnerable group that is the resident staff.

THE INDIGENT PATIENT

A third area that may create a dilemma for the administrative and professional staff with significant implications for the ethical climate of the hospital is policy on the indigent patient. While in the cases of incompetent staff and residency hours, the two cultures may join toward the furtherance of inappropriate ends, on the issue of the indigent patient their basic values often clash.

When hospitals began in the fourth century as a part of a multipurpose space called a hospice, which was set aside in cathedrals for the care of sick and other troubled people, their responsibility toward the needy became established and has remained fixed in the social conscience. This responsibility is shared by medicine and other health care professions.

In the United States, where the prevailing view has historically been that gaining basic life needs is essentially the responsibility of individuals and not the government, hospitals now find themselves under constant pressure to provide more health care than can be fully paid for. The hospital's commitment to survival and its responsibilities for the collective well-being of patients in the community tend to focus its policy on limiting the amount of medical attention given to any one person who lacks the resources to pay. It views as essential the need to keep one eye fixed on today and the other focused on tomorrow. It seeks to balance its obligations to those known persons in need of treatment now and those unknown needy others who will appear at the door in the future. The clinical staff, not encumbered as the hospital is with the expense of tangible goods in providing unreimbursed care (staff basically give time not products to patients), and shaped by ethical commitments to securing the welfare of the patient before them, finds such a balance difficult and often rejects it.

Strategies to meet this problem are available, such as better prognostic criteria, which help allocate expensive therapy according to the value of benefit, and interinstitutional agreements to rationalize the sharing of community resources to meet the needs of the indigent. However, too often hospital policy on care of the indigent patient is set through administrative decision rather than staff and administrative dialogue. Since the hospital and the professional staff both have historically based obligations to care for those who cannot pay, should not hospital policy represent a consensus of the two groups? In many hospitals I have visited, the staff has no clear picture of the basis for hospital policy on indigence.

It is important for administration and professional staff also to recognize a basic limit—they alone cannot provide a solution to the issue of medical indigency. The scope of the problem demands a broad social and national approach. But each hospital can craft policies to allocate resources in a way that best meets the shared vision of its constituents. The critical element is the development of a process which allows a consensus to form about what are appropriate trade-offs. Administration, acting autonomously, should not decide where that point of balance rests. Such problems can be met if the cultures develop arrangements that permit open hospital discussion of interests and values on matters concerning them all and, recognizing mutual dependency as a fundamental aspect of their circumstance, resolve to make consensus the basis of institutional policy.

CONCLUSION

Search committees and boards of hospital trustees involved in choosing institutional leaders should specify as part of the selection process the ability of the person to identify and integrate corporate and professional values in establishing hospital policy. Corporate leaders should recognize their implicit role as teachers of what is valued through the medium of the policies they create and should consider an explicit teaching function—administrative ethics rounds—in which issues of significance to the hospital are presented as cases and discussed with an eye to making recommendations and reaching consensus.

Over the past two decades clinicians have become comfortable in discussing the ethical basis of their medical judgments in open forums before staff. This openness was not purchased easily. Reluctance to place what they considered personal value judgments before public gatherings led to resistance and rejection by many clinicians early in the modern medical ethics movement. However, gradually the saliency of open consideration of all facts relevant to clinical decisions triumphed. Perhaps the time is at hand for the corporate side of medicine to initiate the same open and formal consideration of the ethical values and other factors that are part of making decisions on hospital problems. Why not add administrative ethics rounds to those conducted in the clinical divisions of the hospital such as surgery, medicine, and nursing? Perhaps we should even give to corporate heads of hospitals the additional title, Lecturer on Corporate Values and Actions, to connote the true teaching role that such a position in fact carries and that we expect them to perform.

At the start of the twentieth century, a movement instituted regular exercises among the members of the clinical staff of hospitals that permitted the evaluation of what actually happened through the combined influences of illness and therapy that caused a patient to die. These became known as the weekly mortality conference and the clinico-pathological conference. A tradition thus became established so that making errors or being uncertain was not in itself censurable—but failing to discuss uncertainties or mistakes in order to learn from them was.

In mid-century a second movement arose which asked clinicians to examine the ethical justification that led to therapeutic choices. This has validated the cogency of public discourse on the ethical dimensions of clinical decision making.

Perhaps as this century nears its end we are poised to enter a third era, one where corporate decisions bearing on the ethos of practice and patient care in hospitals can be considered in structured forums in which the multiple values of the institution can be displayed and argued over. Such discussions are one way of attempting to prevent the two cultures of corporation and profession from rending the hospital in half or cooperating without adequate discourse in the pursuit of unworthy ends. Modern technologic medicine cannot exist without the interaction of these two cultures. Coexistence will require dialogue and a commitment to shape policies that do not critically damage either the professional or corporate values so necessary to the vitality of the health care enterprise. Is a humane corporation possible? Events in health care will supply an answer.

NOTES

1. William Mayo, "Contributions of the Nineteenth Century to a Living Pathology," *Boston Medical and Surgical Journal* 167 (1912): 54.
2. Hippocrates, "The Oath," in *Hippocrates*, ed. W. H. S. Jones (Cambridge, Mass.: Harvard University Press, 1923), vol. 1, pp. 164–165.
3. American Medical Association, Principles of Medical Ethics, 1957, in *Ethics in Medicine: Historical Perspectives and Contemporary Concerns*, ed. S. J. Reiser, A. J. Dyck, and W. J. Curran (Cambridge, Mass.: MIT Press, 1977), p. 38.
4. William F. May, "Code and Covenant or Philanthropy and Contract," in ibid., p. 65.

MITCHELL T. RABKIN

THE HOSPITAL—ACADEMIC HEALTH

CENTER INTERFACE: THE COMMUNITY

OF PRACTICE AND THE COMMUNITY

OF LEARNING

Every month or two we hold an orientation session for new employees at Boston's Beth Israel Hospital. I participate and, among other things, welcome the employees and tell them a bit about our philosophy. "Who has been a patient in a hospital, any hospital?" I ask. Invariably there are several who raise their hands and then respond to my further question, "Was it a pleasant experience or not so pleasant?" Virtually always, their responses give me the opportunity to point out that those things which made the experience pleasant most often have little or nothing to do with the technology of care but rather with the human-to-human interactions in which the patient was enmeshed during hospitalization. "Patients are people," I emphasize, "and they have feelings no different from those we would have in similar circumstances." I go on to stress that employees are people too, and our own feelings are almost as vulnerable in our day-to-day interactions at work as are those of the patient. Regardless of which side of the bed we happen to be on, the issue of feelings is important. Thus the goal of the institution is not simply to make it a good place to be if one is a patient, it is also to make the hospital a good place to be if one is an employee. To me, that is a humane environment.

Since humane environments for teaching, inquiry, and healing involve every one of the hospital's employees and medical staff in one way or another, doesn't it mean that the humane environment we seek must take into account the needs of all those involved? Who is involved in the academic health center? Who are the customers? Some would argue patients, others would add physicians and might even put them first. But others are involved as well—all the employees—we are all customers of each other, including all the medical staff, house officers, students, and the board of trustees. It seems to me that a humane environment cannot be achieved unless all of these participants are reassured that their own needs are being respected and responded to. Only then will each be secure and comfortable enough to be able to recognize the needs of others.

I have been asked to focus on the community of practice and the community of learning. Shall we consider practice and learning as abstract notions or as realities made concrete by the needs, aspirations, and goals of the various individuals involved? After all, the way an institution might enhance or minimize potential conflict between values fostering practice and values fostering learning will depend upon how that institution sees itself, that is, as an institution where one set of values is taken to dominate the other or as one where the two sets of values can coexist with minimal tension.

When Beth Israel Hospital was founded, its goals and its self-image were characterized as follows:

> The object of this Corporation shall be to provide medical and hospital services for the sick and disabled of any race, creed, color, or nationality, and to carry on such educational, philanthropic, and scientific activities and functions as are a part of efficient, modern hospital service.

The institution was brought into being by a community which also subscribed to the elevating character of ongoing education. The mission statement was therefore put into effect in a way which continued close identification with the community through responsiveness to patients' needs and respect for their expectations, but which also established the importance of academic achievement.

The statement was subsequently expanded by the Beth Israel board of trustees in 1983:

> The major mission of the Beth Israel Hospital is to deliver patient care of the highest quality, in both scientific and human terms. This mission is to be carried out within a framework of financially responsible management which is sensitive to the requirements both to deliver care which is efficient and cost-effective and to be considerate of the overall health needs of the population of concern to the Hospital.

The sense of community is thus expanded but so are the notions of practice and learning, for the statement goes on to emphasize: "Patient care is to be provided in a context of clinical teaching, through the participation of clinicians, teachers, research scientists, and others who are also the sources of innovation and progress for future improvements in care capabilities" and " . . . the Hospital will continue to exercise leadership through excellence in teaching and research activities as well as in its clinical services." The mix of our physicians is validated; they shall include "those whose primary activities are directed toward the practice of clinical medicine and those whose activities focus primarily upon teaching, research, and more delineated clinical practice. While it is recognized that either group partakes of some of the activities of the other, it is understood that both are essential to the future of Beth Israel Hospital. The continuing productive and complementary relationship of each with the other shall be fostered, within the limits of available resources, in support of the hospital's overall mission."

Many institutions find, however, that such statements declaring that the communities of practice and learning shall beat their swords into plowshares and live side by side are not sufficient to prevent the development of conflict. It may be that there is another, more fundamental ethical issue at the core. I think back on the days, some decades ago, when at certain teaching hospitals in New York City, for example, the emergency unit resident would direct municipal ambulances to reload a patient just delivered to them with an acute myocardial infarction because it was deemed by the resident that the teaching floors already had enough acute myocardial disease at that moment. It was an ethic which apparently judged that the goal of having a broad spectrum of patients available for learning by house staff would not be well served by admitting another MI patient on the floors. Here was a more fundamental issue, not simply one of conflict between practice and learning but also a basic statement on the value of the life of the patients who were surely disadvantaged by the subsequent trip to another hospital and delay in receiving treatment.

On reflection it is not simply the case that one's responsibilities to patients must inevitably override all other institutional and personal commitments. Rather, the basic issue is one of recognition of the many parties involved in the academic medical center—patients, medical staff, house officers, students, employees of all stripes, trustees, the community at large, and those who support the hospital—and among the medical staff, those whose interests lie in clinical medicine and those focused on the laboratory. The basic ethical issue, it seems to me, is to recognize the validity of the needs and goals of each of these components of that complex entity, the academic medical center, and to work to achieve solutions which are most consistent with the institution's mission and which benefit each participant to the greatest extent possible. While it cannot be all things to all people, the institution should not help one component in ways that wreak havoc on another. Piloting the academic medical center—or even pulling on one of its oars—is thus a constant challenge as human needs evolve and yet remain constant, as goals and strivings emerge and economic forces surface and shift, and the balance among all of these swirls kaleidoscopically.

Another way of juxtaposing the communities of practice and learning might be through examining the distinction between illness and disease. Patricia Benner and Judith Wrubel, in their new volume, *The Primacy of Caring*, cite two sets of authors, Cassell and Kleinman, Eisenberg and Good, commenting that "illness is the human experience of loss or dysfunction, whereas disease is the manifestation of aberration at the tissue, cellular, or organ levels." Perhaps pure scholarship can deal with the notion of disease completely separated from the individual, able to be viewed with no immediate human consequences following from the leisure taken in a purely academic approach to disease. Illness, on the other hand, involves human beings, not only as the disease moves into a real person but in the imperfect world enmeshing both patients and practitioners, a world made vulnerable by the lack of perfect information, by the pressures of time and the need for commitment to diagnostic and therapeutic actions in order to benefit the patient. Accepting these notions of disease and illness, each a part of the basic rhythm of the academic medical center, we face the challenge to get on with it, to forge the link between the community of practice and the community of learning as only one of the challenges we face in order to meet the needs and goals of all who make up the academic health center.

There was such a tradition at Beth Israel Hospital before I arrived in 1966. We were known as a reasonably warm place which paid attention to patients yet strived for academic excellence and seemed able to achieve both to a modest degree or better. If we have strengthened this sense over the last twenty-three years, it has happened largely through actions taken for their own sake, pointing to one or another goal appropriate to the academic medical center, actions consciously consistent with our philosophy of accommodation whose consequences were usually thoughtfully projected, but not actions taken simply to strengthen the visibility of our commitment to harmony between learning and practice. Our leaders identify with achievement but by their achievements build the entire organization. I cannot emphasize strongly enough the importance of these role models in defining what an institution stands for. By their visible actions, people embody philosophy. You can declaim forever but actions speak far louder than words.

In my beginnings at Beth Israel, there were some very simple examples of such actions. Seeing to it that the name badges for everyone from waste handler to chief of service were identical reinforced the basic notion of the intrinsic equal worth of each individual as part of the team. In 1972, Beth Israel became the first hospital to publish a statement on the rights of patients. Simply put, it says that the patient has the right to be treated with dignity and respect, the patient has the right to know what is happening to him or her, and if the patient feels that these rights are not being respected, he or she has the right to blow the whistle and we will take the time and trouble to respond in a helpful manner. Some expressed doubts at the time, concerns that such a forthright invitation might bring all sorts of crazies out of the woodwork, but none emerged. In general, where patients insisted upon the letter of the rights statement being followed, they were more often correct and we stood to learn about the productive partnership of patient and provider. Subsequently, the concept of patients' rights has become widespread.

Another major example of action consistent with our philosophy of accommodation has been the development of primary nursing at Beth Israel. While the phrase *primary nursing* may have different meanings to different groups of nurses, in our venue primary nursing places the professional nurse at the bedside, with true responsibility for decision making on many aspects of understanding and dealing with the patient's illness, as well as the opportunity to monitor the overall progress of the patient and coordinate the work of nurses and other care givers with the intentions and efforts of the patient's physician. Some physicians initially resented having to seek out the primary nurse assigned to any one particular patient, but they soon became convinced that the effort was worth it since the information the physician now received about the patient's course was infinitely better, the care considerably improved, and the satisfaction of the patient visibly heightened. Equally important to the institution was the fact that the professionalism of the nurse's role increased dramatically. Many changes in other nursing roles—those of the head nurse and above—also followed, with a remarkable upswing in the gratification derived from working as a Beth Israel nurse and, as a logical consequence, a significant growth in the desire of nurses nationwide to work at Beth Israel. Again, the underlying emphasis was not simply that patients had needs which should be fulfilled, but rather that our existing systems left much to be desired for patients, nurses, and physicians as well. Our concepts of the needs of each enlarged; it was not a victory of one over the other. And the results speak for themselves.

It is not simple to relate how this philosophy became established at Beth Israel as a part of its fundamental fabric. It is easier to say that I and those others who followed the founders share their philosophy; the founders built the works and we now keep the flywheel going. Communications are critical in that regard. Virtually every week I write a one- or two-page newsletter—the "Dear Doctor" letter—which is directed to medical staff, top administration, and the board of trustees, and another—the "Employee Newsletter"—which everyone receives. The subject matter ranges from mundane alerts that the garage roof will be closed for repairs to editorial comments on hospital or outside events. With the arrival of new house staff there is an annual reiteration of two basic questions, always to be put in the following order: how can we help the patient? In doing so, what can we learn?

Letters from patients—generally of commendation—are reproduced and so, occasionally, are criticisms (such as the overhearing of a conversation between two physicians on the elevator—comments which should have been kept to more private circumstances). Just as Coca-Cola never stops advertising, we never stop beating the drum. But we always try to refrain from sanctimony and the sense of "having it made." Particularly in a service industry one has to run scared, since yesterday's good service counts for little today, and no amount of good care can be stored on the shelves for the days when demand is particularly pressing.

There are other ways in which the philosophy of the institution is voiced and reinforced. Letters to me—again, mostly of praise but not always—are answered invariably by me. The letter and reply are shared with the individuals involved and their managers so that commendable actions are reinforced through recognition. When the letter contains criticism, the incident is investigated. The reply might range from agreement that we did drop the ball, in which case we extend our apologies, to the other extreme of an unjust criticism which signifies a patient or family with an inappropriate sense of entitlement. In that instance, the reply demonstrates to the hospital personnel involved how to deal with such a criticism without being defensive or acceding to unreasonable demands, yet in a manner consistent with our professional responsibilities to patient and family.

In the recounting, dilemmas dealt with yesterday somehow seem much simpler than those we confront today, and the tensions between the communities of practice and learning seem only to heighten. While the situation may vary from state to state, the growing press of economic retrenchment will sensitize the conflict. So will new regulatory efforts concerned with matters such as house officers' hours and various reporting requirements. At the academic medical center the issue arises anew each time there is a search for a department chair, particularly in medicine, surgery, or one of the other major specialties. The academic search committee may feel its most important preparatory task is to predict where the specialty will be going over the next decade or two. However, for the success of the new chair, it is probably even more important to reexamine the basic values of the institution as a whole and determine where it is heading so that the candidate can know what he or she will be walking into and be given the opportunity to understand and commit to the institution's mission and goals in advance. Surely the most successful of chiefs are those who, in addition to their virtues in practice and in learning, have said, in effect, "I see the banner under which this academic health center marches, I like it, I subscribe to it. I'll join the team."

Today at Beth Israel, we're involved in another most interesting experiment concerned with delineation of values. We are pressed by third party payers for more prudence in expenditures, yet driven internally to seek greater capability in diagnosis and treatment. We thus feel the growing emphasis upon economy and productivity but also see the need to maintain quality, for the latter is beginning to come under assault as third party funds are held back. The continual bombardment we face—restrictions, denials, and the like—has its impact on the morale of physicians, nurses, and all employees. This is particularly important in a service industry—and hospitals surely are a service industry—where dispirited employees respond far less well to the legitimate demands of their customers, whether patients, doctors, or each other. Inevitably, we will be confronted with more and more requirements, often in conflict with others we must also take on. We must moderate expenditures, yet improve productivity in an increasingly stressful environment. We must sustain and even improve the quality of care. And we should maintain that optimistic outlook which allows us to reach out and comfort the afflicted without fail.

Toward those ends, top management at Beth Israel looked at both service and manufacturing industries and found a program in participative management. The Scanlon Plan is an effort to revise the sociology of the workplace, one which has been successful in a number of manufacturing businesses but was never before tried in the service sector, to the best of my knowledge. It is a program of participative management and gainsharing developed by Joseph Scanlon, first a steelworker and then an academician at MIT. Scanlon felt that most workers in industry were well motivated and could be a powerful force for good but required circumstances which nourished that motivation. The good to be sought was greater productivity and improved quality at lower cost. What employees needed to achieve those goals, he felt, was to be kept knowledgeable about how the company was doing—in the marketplace and in relation to its own budget and bottom line—and also knowledgeable about how each worker's own area related to the company's success. Employees so informed would be motivated to identify impediments to greater productivity and find ways to improve quality and cut costs. This motivation could be effective only if employees had a ready mechanism to voice their ideas for improvement in a manner which avoided the turf issues and other interpersonal barriers that often seem to blockade suggested improvement and an equally ready mechanism to implement the good ideas thereby derived. Scanlon also argued that the benefits resulting from these employee efforts should be recognized through a mechanism allowing both employees and the company to share in any material gain.

In our academic medical center, these ideas seem to make sense. The notion of workers (I use the term generically to encompass both nonmedical employees and medical staff) in the hospital "owning" the problems of productivity and quality and cost control has become an important goal. We reasoned that if employees at Beth Israel already owned the problem of projecting warmth and personal concern toward patients and visitors while maintaining their commitment to technical excellence—and they do—perhaps we could find a way to deal with the matters of productivity and quality with a comparable measure of success. Toward those ends, we have been engaged in a major, hospital-wide effort, first educating employees, then medical staff, and finally trustees; then developing the essentials of our own Scanlon Plan; and now, finally, beginning the full-scale implementation. We call it PREPARE/21, symbolizing our determination to prepare Beth Israel for the twenty-first century.

I mention this effort not to proclaim success or even to profess the virtue of Boston's Beth Israel Hospital, but rather to underscore some of the challenges confronting the academic medical center with its tensions between the demands of care and those of learning. We are attempting to foster, once again, recognition and fulfillment of the needs and goals of all parties concerned, to assign credibility to them all (though all may not have the same weight), and to open a pathway of optimal achievement for all. We have introduced the concept of equity, not only in the conventional sense of fair treatment for all parties but in the sense that each of the parties involved in the academic medical center makes an investment in the institution simply by virtue of participation. And for that investment there is legitimate expectation of return. For patients investing their lives, there is the expectation of prompt, capable, and efficient treatment, which is at the same time kind and thoughtful. For physicians the return begins with a system that works efficiently to support their care of the patients. There is also the expectation of appropriate opportunities for career advancement, whether as clinicians or in research and teaching. For other hospital employees the expectation is one of equitable treatment, a pleasant place to work, fair pay, opportunities for advancement, and personal respect. For trustees it is the assurance of a stable place of excellence available to the community in times of need.

There is a harmony in this notion of equity, in the idealization of this participative management plan, whose further details are beyond the scope of this paper. But note: in the document we have published which outlines PREPARE/21, there is a statement on the rights of employees and staff and, as with our earlier broadside on patients' rights, a listing of the responsibilities as well. There are the rights to be informed about the realities the hospital faces, to help shape the directions the hospital will take to sustain and strengthen its excellence, and to participate in setting one's own work-specific goals in order to make possible new achievements which will strengthen the institution. We conclude: "Committed to these rights and accepting the responsibilities and opportunities which accompany them, Beth Israel employees and staff will work to develop and manage new ways to sustain and improve our patient care, research, and teaching, and to carry out all the other activities appropriate to our role as a leader among hospitals."

I'm afraid I may not have provided much substance toward resolving the conflict between the worlds of practice and scholarship. What I have attempted to do, however, is to convey my sense that the approach, if not the solution, is twofold. First, the basic philosophy of the institution must be articulated clearly and unequivocally. The distinction must be made between invited conflict and a healthy tension among different approaches toward a common goal. Then, the focus must be on *process*, process which day after day strengthens the institution's philosophy and goals and exemplifies its way of life. It is a series of successive approximations, I believe, and each step provides perhaps as many insights into our naïveté in hoping to achieve the goals as it may in narrowing the gap between the real and the ideal. Process and successive approximation to the ideal are what count, and the constancy of effort and the visible banner at the head of the column are the keys to forward movement. It is that simple and that complex.

JAMES G. HAUGHTON

DETERMINANTS OF THE

CULTURE AND PERSONALITY

OF INSTITUTIONS

E very institution has its own personality, whether it is a business, a
church, or a hospital. That personality is determined by the culture
of the institution, and the culture of the institution is determined by
the nature of the people in it. It is often asserted that the leader of an
organization creates its personality and culture. But that is true only to
the extent that the leader can determine the several parameters which
define the institution:
1. What will be its product or service?
2. Who will be its clientele?
3. What will be its location?
4. Who will be its personnel?
If these characteristics are beyond the control of the leadership, its
ability to determine the personality of the institution, while still substantial, will be limited.
 Consider a few examples. In Los Angeles there is a street called Rodeo
Drive. It is perhaps the most famous, exclusive, and expensive shopping
enclave in the United States. On that street is an institution which has
become internationally famous. It is named for its owner who has determined that his establishment should be among the most expensive,
exclusive, and well known in the United States if not the world. He has
therefore chosen the most prestigious location, offers the most diverse
and expensive merchandise available, and provides such unique ser-

vices as shopping by appointment. To assure that his unique clientele receives unique service, he has carefully selected and trained his staff in keeping with his goals. He has thus determined the personality of his enterprise.

There are universities in our country whose leaders have defined the culture of their individual institutions by selecting locations, choosing faculty, establishing specific entrance requirements, and providing certain academic offerings. These decisions define the culture of the organization because they determine the people who will make up the academic community, that is, its faculty, staff, and students. This definition of the institution's culture determines its personality. Will it be an elitist institution accepting predominantly students who come from the most prestigious prep schools? Will its students be predominantly self-taught because its prestigious faculty is more committed to its research agenda than to teaching? These institutional descriptions and questions may be applied to characteristics perceived to be positive, but are equally valid when the characteristics are thought to be negative.

In the private sector, the owners or leaders of an organization can exercise a great deal of influence over its culture and personality, as they can decide whether to serve an affluent or a financially deprived clientele. That decision determines the nature of the merchandise to be offered, the location of the enterprise, the nature of the staff to be hired, the training provided to them, and the standards of conduct demanded of them. In the arena of medical care these considerations become extremely critical because they not only define the prospective patients, they also affect the outcomes of our therapeutic efforts.

The location of a hospital substantially influences the nature of the population that it will serve. Its sponsorship—private investor–owned, private nonprofit, public—influences the clientele that it will seek, the staff that it will select, and the services that it will offer. Location, thus, becomes a part of the sponsorship equation.

In the private sector almost all of these decisions are within the control of the corporate leaders. Marketing strategies are designed to attract the most prestigious physicians who will bring the best-financed patients; services offered are those most generously supported by available financing mechanisms; amenities offered are those designed to please the desired clientele. For example, in one southwestern city a private hospital provides valet parking for patients and visitors to enhance the caring image of the institution. Such signals from the leadership send a clear message to all levels of staff that the patient must be accorded every courtesy, and the orientation provided to staff will usually stress the policy that failure to display behavior which reflects the desired personality of the institution will result in negative outcomes to staff.

The public sector provides quite a different set of opportunities for leaders to define the culture and personality of their institutions. In the United States, history and tradition have determined that publicly financed health and medical care services are intended for the financially and medically needy. That determination usually dictates that the institution will be located in an economically depressed urban area, since access is thus enhanced for its target population. The location imperative, however, brings its own problems. Security in such a location, for both patients and staff, will almost certainly be a concern. A threatening location has the dual effect of assuring that almost all patients will be those forced by financial disadvantage to use these services and limiting the pool of staff, both professional and support, from which recruiting can occur. The problem is well illustrated by three examples taken from the three largest cities in the United States in three different decades.

In the 1960s in New York City it was difficult to recruit professional staff to Lincoln Hospital in the South Bronx because the area was perceived to be dangerous. But to serve the poor in the Bronx, it was necessary for Lincoln Hospital to be located there. In the 1970s in Chicago it was similarly difficult to recruit nurses and other professional staff to Cook County Hospital because the West Side was perceived to be dangerous. But to serve the poor of Chicago, it was necessary for the hospital to be in that spot. In the late 1980s in Los Angeles, it was difficult to recruit nurses to work at the King/Drew Medical Center in the heart of the South Central Los Angeles "war zone," where drive-by shootings with assault rifles were a daily occurrence. But to serve the financially deprived population of South Central Los Angeles the medical center had to be located there.

It also follows that because minority populations are overrepresented among the poor, the clientele served by such institutions will be predominantly ethnic minorities. Because of location and public sponsorship, most of the support and ancillary staff and some of the medical, nonmedical, and administrative professional staff will be of minority background and financially deprived origin.

These realities present a unique and demanding set of challenges to the leadership of such an institution in defining its personality and culture. The administrator and medical director of the hospital would like the institution to be perceived as a caring, humane, and efficient organization. But without real control of the parameters previously mentioned, the task is enormous. They usually cannot change the location of the institution and would not if they could. Thus the recruitment pool for staff is severely limited. This limitation is further exaggerated by a political factor: because such institutions, in addition to being sources of medical care, are also major sources of employment in these communities, there is substantial community pressure to recruit all levels of staff from that community and its predominant ethnic group.

The following examples may be denied and even resented by some, but they represent real life depictions of the human interactions which occur in these settings.

Young black or hispanic persons who are now registered nurses, physicians, senior administrators, or social workers with master's degrees may have been the first members of their families to attend college or even finish high school. They may have grown up in low-income housing developments among drug dealers, prostitutes, and ne'er-do-wells. But because of their determination and courage they have escaped from this morass and emerged as professionals serving their community but living apart from it. All of the poor, unlettered patients of the same ethnic background who come under the care of these persons are not only reminders of their own beginnings but can be a source of embarrassment or a cause of resentment to these professionals because the patients have failed to pull themselves out of the quagmire as the staff did. This combination of very human feelings can make the staff members professionally judgmental, punitive, and less than humane in delivering services to such patients.

Or consider the receptionist, clerk, or nurse's aide who not only comes from such a background but still lives in it and still suffers the indignities that such an environment inflicts daily on its residents. The only difference between those staff members and their patients is that they have obtained employment in this publicly funded institution and are not receiving public assistance. Such members of the staff experience the same rage that is the constant companion of the disenfranchised. When such an employee is confronted with the rudeness and aggression of a patient in physical and emotional pain, it is the natural tendency to respond in kind regardless of the efforts of the hospital leadership to engender a caring, courteous personality for the institution.

This portrayal of the realities of human interactions within the institution suggests that in order to achieve the personality to which the institution aspires, the leadership must not only provide training and policies which encourage caring but must also recognize the need of staff for counseling and support, encouragement, and understanding of the stress under which they constantly function.

Another phenomenon of the last two decades also tends to define the culture of hospitals. During that time the nursing profession has emerged from the shadow of the physician and nurses are no longer seen as the physicians' servants. The push for professional independence has led to the demand for independent practice and billing. This movement has succeeded substantially outside the hospital, but in many hospitals nursing continues to view itself as unappreciated and disrespected. In such hospitals nurses and physicians behave as members of two separate armed camps with a chasm between them. It is usually the patient who falls into the chasm.

Consider a scenario in which a young physician in training writes an order for a patient. The nurse assigned to that patient believes that the order is improper and out of concern for her or his own professional licensure does not carry it out. Because of the antipathy between nurses and doctors in the hospital the nurse is not comfortable bringing the perceived medical error to the attention of the trainee, the attending physician, or the chief of service. As a result the patient goes without medication for a day or two until his or her condition deteriorates or utilization review uncovers the fact that no care is being provided.

This scenario is not a fantasy. It actually happens, and it presents a serious challenge to the leadership of hospitals when it exists. The fact that in the public sector nurses usually consider themselves to be underpaid serves to reinforce their perception that they are not appreciated or respected.

The physical environment in which care takes place sends its own messages to patients and staff. Almost twenty years ago I was invited to serve as executive director of the newly created Health and Hospitals Governing Commission of Cook County. On my very first visit to Chicago for an interview with the newly appointed board, I was taken on a tour of Cook County Hospital. As I walked through the dingy hallways and the thirty- to forty-bed wards, some without privacy curtains, I knew exactly what I would do to lift the morale of the obviously dispirited staff if I accepted the position. Several weeks later when my tenure as executive director began I took three simple steps. One, I hired a former master sergeant who upon his retirement from the military had entered the hotel industry and become an executive housekeeper. I made him head of the hospital's housekeeping department to put that army of ex–patronage workers to work cleaning up the hospital, stripping and waxing the floors, washing old blood stains and spills from the walls, and removing dust from windowsills and fixtures for years untouched. Two, I selected a team of architectural designers to plan the renovation and decoration of the hospital. Three, after a new color scheme was designed, I immediately let loose a horde of painters in the hallways, wards, clinics, and offices of the buildings. Within six months the buildings, though sixty years old, were sparkling with bright colors, shiny floors, and clean windows and the morale of staff and patients soared.

I took these steps because in a previous experience in another city, while visiting a hospital under my jurisdiction, I had chided a young resident for his uncaring attitude toward a patient. His response to my counseling was: "Doctor, look at this place. If this city wanted me to provide good care to these people, they wouldn't put me to work in a place that looks like this." I looked around at the walls that had not been painted for many years, the dirty floors, and the crowded spaces and knew that he was right.

Take a look at the way your residents dress. I have often been told by public attorneys that we cannot impose dress codes on our young doctors. But several years ago in one of our public hospitals, I saw a patient with a tuberculous cavity in her lung. She had been seen in the emergency room six months earlier and had been referred to the pulmonary clinic for care. She had not returned in spite of efforts to reach her. When asked why, she responded, "I didn't like the doctor." When asked why she did not like the doctor she said, "He was wearing dirty sneakers." Clearly the resident's view of how poor people expect their doctors to look varied substantially from the patient's view. Since then we have encouraged appropriate professional dress in spite of the attorneys.

Some of these concerns may seem inconsequential. But to our patients these issues display the personality of the institution and convey messages that may adversely affect the compliance of our patients in spite of our superior medical expertise. Because academic health centers so frequently function in the public sector where we cannot select the physical and human environment, these considerations must be of particular concern to us. Our control over the factors which define the culture of our organizations is often limited, but we should not allow that to deter us from defining and leading our institutions to the efficient, supportive, and caring personalities that our patients deserve.

LAWRENCE W. GREEN

THE REVIVAL OF COMMUNITY

AND THE PUBLIC OBLIGATION

OF ACADEMIC HEALTH CENTERS

For at least two decades now my generation has been lamenting and mourning the passing of the community as we knew it when we were younger. Some of our favorite films and books have been nostalgic depictions of bygone communities, such as Larry McMurtry's *The Last Picture Show* and Garrison Keillor's *Lake Wobegon Days*.[1] Of course, people have always gravitated to literature and art that captured the mood, the tempo, or the memories of their lost youth. Disneyland's Main Street and three-quarter scale put everything in its proper place and proper size. In this perspective of community, the academic health center would be a group of family doctors with mortar boards.

But *Dallas, Miami Vice, L.A. Law, Mississippi Burning,* and *St. Elsewhere* present us with new, unsettling images of the community of today and recent decades. Have the character and vitality of communities really changed? Or have we romanticized the past and mistaken growth, specialization, increasing complexity, and the greater visibility of our problems for decline and decay? Whether communities are still in decline or reviving, what can academic health centers contribute to the protection and promotion of their health through community education, primary care, and technical assistance?

The media image of the academic health center, especially the hospital as depicted by *St. Elsewhere*, is of an embattled fortress patching up the wounded victims of violently collapsing communities, but not really working *in* the community to help it build and maintain its health, safety, and quality of life. The university, in general, remains peripheral to community life in the minds of most Americans. Even the recent accounts of the role of universities in community social change in the 1960s seem to be rewritten in unflattering and uninspiring terms.[2] Leighton E. Cluff, president of the Robert Wood Johnson Foundation, spoke in a recent interview of his experience as a watcher of academic health centers:

> I have not been impressed with their ability to grapple with some of the critically important health problems of populations or communities . . . I find it disturbing personally to visit a medical school or an academic health center in an area where there are serious problems with substance abuse, suicide, sexually transmitted diseases, and services for the elderly, only to learn that the institutions are ignoring these problems. Medical schools pursue their interests in magnetic resonance imaging and computerized axial tomography scanning, in molecular biology, and in rare diseases, but they are not paying a hell of a lot of attention to the major problems of their own communities.[3]

This superficial sweep of history, public health, and community organization will be biased by the communities I have known in my personal odyssey from Berkeley and Bangladesh in the 1960s, to Baltimore and Washington in the 1970s, to Boston and Houston and back to the Bay Area in the 1980s. My purpose is to reflect on the changing place of community in the promotion and protection of health and the place of the academic health center in community development for health. This is important to university faculty and staff not only as citizens of communities themselves, but as professionals whose life work is devoted to improving the well-being of people where they live. The task of academic health centers is to affect science, policies, and practices that will serve the health of people better. My thesis is that they can accomplish these tasks with greater relevance, effectiveness, and reach if they become more integral to community life—just as integral as hospitals were a generation ago and family doctors were a generation before that.

THE HISTORICAL CONTEXT

When Alexis de Tocqueville, in 1831, characterized American democracy as active participation by ordinary citizens in the associations and movements of community life, he was looking at a society whose central institutions were still taking form, whose far-flung frontiers were expanding, and whose communities were therefore dynamic and relatively self-sufficient.[1] Communities existed in America before government. People had to be active in community affairs on the frontier for they had no formal government to act for them. The federal attitude followed the Jeffersonian view: "That society governs best that governs least."

When Abraham Lincoln, in 1862, signed the Land Grant Act creating the great state universities that house many of the academic health centers today, he saw the need for the centralization of science and technological resources at least to the state level because of the need for a critical mass, but he also intended that the universities be highly accessible in their research and educational functions to the communities of their regions. A degree of centralization was necessary, but service to local communities was the intent. The Federalist attitude here was that of James Madison, "Knowledge will forever govern ignorance; and a people who mean to be their own Governors must arm themselves with the power which knowledge gives."

When another Abraham named Flexner sixty-five years later recommended the revamping of medical schools to put greater emphasis on science, he viewed their role as national and international in scope rather than regional or local.

As universities and their professional schools in academic health centers became increasingly global in their orientation, communities were becoming more and more dependent on resources beyond their control. From the self-sufficient farming communities of colonial America to the single-industry towns of the westward expansion and the industrial revolution to the Silicon Valleys of today's information and service industry era, communities have become increasingly dependent on other communities and on higher levels of organization and government to facilitate, coordinate, and regulate their interdependence. The academic health center in this context becomes as much a broker of health resources to the community as a provider. While communities were turning increasingly outward for health resources and services, academic health centers were influenced more and more by federal regulations and funding rather than community needs.

The Constitution of the United States never intended that much power and authority for human services be placed at the federal level. The Constitution makes no mention of health, for example. Only where interstate commerce or international relations were at issue could the federal government justify intervention on community health, education, and welfare problems. (A minister of education in France once looked at his watch and announced to his American visitor that he could tell him exactly what every pupil in France was studying at that moment and what book they were using. The American, obviously, was at a loss to match this feat of omniscience.) But even with our pluralism, the growing interdependence of communities in this century has brought us at least five megatrends (to borrow Naisbitt's concept but not the same trends):

1. Highly developed and centralized resources in our national institutions and organizations, leaving communities less able to meet the needs of their own citizens and control technical resources

2. A continuing concentration and sprawl of population and wealth in the largest metropolitan areas, leaving smaller communities more resource poor, and individual citizens in central urban core areas more alienated

3. Mass communications, jet travel, electronic technologies, and global economies all making local communities less autonomous, less self-sufficient

4. Vertical structures of bottom-up reporting and loyalty from local organizations to their central headquarters at state and national levels, making horizontal commitments to other local organizations or to the community more difficult

5. Vertical structures of top-down categorical funding for health and other social service programs from central organizations to local organizations who are required to adhere to central rules and to accept limitations on local discretion and decision making

All these contemporary circumstances blur the vision of America de Tocqueville described in the nineteenth century. They would seem to make communities and academic health centers the last place one would want to start important programs today. One might even question the wisdom of trying to convert or transfer national innovations and resources through academic health centers into community action. We now seem to have the technologies and institutional structures to communicate directly from central headquarters to individuals in their homes, schools, and workplaces. We can bypass the sluggish machinery and weary bureaucrats in state and local organizations, including academic health centers.

THE CROSSROADS

The question now is whether we should acknowledge the passing of community, local organization, and academic health centers as viable players in the lives of modern Americans and get on with the business of sharpening our skills at communicating *ex cathedra* from Washington, New York, and Hollywood, from corporate headquarters and from state capitals, directly to individuals. Or should we rejoice at the homogenization of the "global village,"[5] embrace the apparent efficiencies and economies of scale in centralized decision making and resource allocation, and exploit the possible opportunity to assure greater equity across geographic regions and communities inherent in centralized control?

Should academic health centers leave it to the Harvard Medical Letter, the Berkeley Wellness Letter, the University of Texas Lifetime Health Letter, Tim Johnson, and Red Duke to do all their communicating with their local communities for them? Should academic health centers leave it to Washington and to state agencies to decide what the configuration of health resources and programs will be in their communities? Or is there a third course academic health centers should steer, neither lamenting nor rejoicing, but accepting the new circumstance as a challenge to forge new ways of working with and channeling resources and ideas through community organizations, institutions, and families on their way to individuals? Would they be bucking a tide of change that is inexorable and irreversible? Or is there a remnant of local spirit and autonomy, an impulse for self-sufficiency and self-determination that won't die and will rise again with the proper nourishment? Indeed, is it possible that it *is* rising again and we need to adapt our centralizing tendencies to respond to this growing demand for decentralized participation?

I believe that interest in local autonomy and participation in self-governance has been reborn, if it was ever dead. The revival of community spirit can be witnessed most dramatically in the two features of American democracy that de Tocqueville considered most central to its special vitality: volunteerism and organizational memberships.

In 1988, Independent Sector commissioned a Gallup poll to assess the state of giving in America. Almost half of all American adults contribute time to a cause, most saying they are giving more time than ever. The average volunteer gives 4.7 hours a week. This amounted to a total of 19.5 billion hours in 1987, which translates roughly to ten million full-time employees.[6] For instance, consider the following facts:

Some 105,000 new service organizations were born between 1982 and 1987 in the United States. Most of these originated as local, not national organizations.[7]

Between 1980 and 1988, the number of community (neighborhood) associations grew from 55,000 to 133,000. More than one in eight Americans (29.4 million people) live in common-interest communities governed by community associations with officials elected by the neighborhood.[8]

Similar explosive growth of medical self-help groups, advocacy groups concerned with the health effects of environmental pollution, exercise groups, weight control groups, and membership organizations of all kinds has signaled a revival of local affiliation, affinity, and collective action.[9]

A *Fortune* survey of business leaders found that they expect to see "radically decentralized organizations" in the 1990s.[10]

How should we interpret these trends? If volunteerism has been so infused with new life, and new community service organizations have been created in such unprecedented numbers, we can either wring our hands over these as signs of the decline and failure of federal programs, or we can seize upon these as signs of revival of community spirit, community self-reliance, and community problem-solving. They are both. True, Ronald Reagan's New Federalism and block grant policies put considerable strain on state and local government to pick up the pieces of dismantled federal programs. True, much of that strain was passed on to academic health centers, voluntary organizations, and families and individual volunteers and meant longer hours and more burnout for the most conscientious human service professionals. True, many people fell through the tattered safety net.

THREE INGREDIENTS OF COMMUNITY

But the circumstances created by these hardships and inequities might also contain the seeds of a new opportunity to revive the three things that communities once offered people: a sense of community, which is a feeling of belonging and a shared sense of responsibility for each other's welfare;[11] the person-to-person touch of neighborhood-based services (high touch above high tech; storefront, horizontal close-to-home services rather than vertical bureaucratically organized services); and the capability of communities to analyze and solve their own problems and to pursue their own ambitions through collective action where individuals alone might feel helpless.

These three ingredients represent the antidotes to the three poisons of industrial civilization: alienation, dehumanization, and disempowerment. Academic health centers can possibly contribute more to health by addressing these dimensions of health care and community development than by putting more resources into the "temples of the medicine men."[12] These are the underlying elements of community health promotion and disease prevention.

What are the roots of the three problems, and how can academic health centers help deliver the antidotes?

ALIENATION VS. SENSE OF COMMUNITY

The loss of a sense of belonging has crept up on Americans with their high levels of competition and geographic mobility. Smaller countries like Japan, Taiwan, and the European countries manage to foster competition without much geographic mobility. But it is more than size of country that accounts for our mobility, for Australia and Canada, both comparable in size, have much less geographic job changing than the United States. In many fields, willingness to move horizontally is a faster way to move vertically up the career ladder. The range of opportunities opened with mobility is greater in the U.S., not because of its geographic size but because of its population size with concomitantly larger numbers of large cities and universities and hospitals. All this makes for a state of perpetual uprootedness for many if not most Americans. We move an average of twelve times in a lifetime, according to the Census Bureau.

This mobility conspires against individuals having a sense of community where they live and, to a lesser extent, where they work. This produces alienation. A study of factors correlated with expert ratings of a sense of community, however, found that the actual duration of residence is less powerful as a predictor of a sense of community than how long an individual *plans* to reside in the community.[13] The three most powerful predictors were amount of interaction with neighbors, level of close neighbor relations, and a sense of civic duty. This suggests that we can generate a sense of belonging even in the most recent newcomers to a community if they can be engaged significantly with their neighbors and with civic responsibilities.

Relationships with neighbors probably declined with the advent of air conditioners. People used to sit on their front porches or stoops to cool off, exchanging greetings with neighbors passing by. The automobile took most of the pedestrians off the sidewalk, which made sitting on the porch less interesting; the television made sitting inside more interesting. Then came the architectural innovation of backyard decks, virtually replacing front porches. Backyard fences replaced the clothesline which once brought neighbors face to face.

Drug dealing in the neighborhood has made the front porch even dangerous. Witness the outpouring of new commitment to community action from alienated and frustrated black professionals and parents leaving the April 1989 first national conference on the black family and crack cocaine. Unlike the 1960s, when black leaders and communities pulled together in the struggle for jobs and equality, the 1970s and early 1980s seem to have been marked by a growing sense of hopelessness that has prompted young blacks to war against each other. Now the crack cocaine and gang warfare crises seem to be precipitating in the minority communities what has been happening more vaguely and subtly in the majority communities. Conditions of living in some minority communities have been so oppressive that a defensive reaction mounted on any single front seemed to be outflanked. Now the drug and gang war situation has so outraged many of these communities that they are issuing their own internal call to action to combat the enemy within, to draw upon the historical pinnacles of black culture and strength—the family and the church—and to mobilize these in the service of neighborhood and community concerns.

When I joined the Johns Hopkins Medical Institutions in 1970, the surrounding neighborhood looked like a bombed-out Dresden at the end of World War II. The urban riots following Martin Luther King's assassination in the late 1960s had left the academic health center a naked fortress in the middle of East Baltimore. During my ten years there the neighborhood seemed mostly to fall into further disrepair. But there were stirrings of cooperation between the Hopkins faculty and community groups. Some of us worked through an innovation called the Mayor's Stations, which were comprehensive service centers located in neighborhoods where a resident could walk for one-stop social and health services short of acute medical care. When I drove up Madison Avenue recently to visit friends at Hopkins I was struck by how much those inner-city neighborhoods of East Baltimore had risen from the ashes. The same pattern can be seen around Temple in Philadelphia and around the Morehouse School of Medicine in Atlanta. Whether these academic health centers had much to do with it or not, a patchwork of reborn neighborhoods can be found in many of the worst-hit cities of the late sixties. Some of it is gentrification, yes, but much of it is pride and patience among an indigenous population learning how to work with their local government and their academic neighbors.

Much more has been written about the family than about the community, especially in recent years with the near extinction of the Norman Rockwell ideal of a working father, a stay-at-home mother, and 2.7 children. Senator Pat Schroeder blames community changes for the assault on the family, especially for the pressure on women to work outside the home ("every mother is a working mother").[14] One could argue this the other way around: that the divorce rate and decline in the family as an institution have weakened community insofar as people have less reason to stay in their communities of birth when their family of birth is dissolved and dispersed. Perhaps the rebirth of communities has had to await the shakedown of families to see what kind of new forms of family would emerge as the foundation for new forms of community cohesion. Eric Foner points out in his book *Reconstruction: America's Unfinished Revolution, 1863–1877* that the South had to go through a *deconstruction* of slavery before it could accomplish reconstruction.[15] Perhaps we have had to endure a deconstruction of the traditional family structure and housebound wives (like slaves?) before we could get on with the reconstruction of community.

The academic health center can contribute much to the reconstruction of the American family and thereby to the redevelopment of a sense of community by putting its own house in order. By developing model programs for its employees that put the family and community involvement above some of the other economic values that now drive employment conditions for staff and faculty, the academic health center could demonstrate to other community employers how such humane programs can benefit the institution, reduce turnover and absenteeism, increase productivity, and improve morale. Daycare programs, work site health promotion programs and facilities, release time for community service, credit for voluntary service in the community, and access of academic health center facilities to community groups can provide employees with a greater sense of commitment to the employer, the community, and the family. Everybody wins.

Academic health centers should be among the innovators in these kinds of progressive policies for employees, demonstrating their health benefits as well as their value to the community and to the employers. Instead, many academic health centers are among the most regressive employers in their communities, exploiting interns and residents with inhumane hours, others with low pay and working conditions that give little or no consideration to family or community attachments.

DEHUMANIZATION VS. NEIGHBORHOOD-BASED SERVICES

The lost sense of belonging to a community was compounded by a lost sense of personal touch with sources of support close to home. Large institutions replaced family and church in many ways. People turned increasingly to governmental, private, and commercial sources for recreation, social support, intellectual stimulation, and social and health services. Some complain that the growth and centralization of governmental bureaucracies and service industries have made the services less personal, less responsive to individual needs, and more perfunctory. These dehumanizing tendencies of formalized service systems have spawned a generation of self-help organizations, some anti-establishment, some merely designed to complement the established systems of services.

Academic health centers can join hands with these proliferating self-help and storefront service organizations to provide more decentralized, personalized services closer to the homes and workplaces of community residents. Academic health centers can provide space, facilities, and leadership to some of these organizations without coopting them, if faculty and staff are encouraged to do so. The reward system for faculty in most places discourages and even penalizes community outreach and involvement. Consultation to federal agencies gets more points in the tenure and promotion process than consultation to community agencies. Service to the top management of large community organizations is considered worthy of the time of university faculty, but not much credit accrues to the academic health center member who reaches out to the small organizations and neighborhood groups.

Daniel Steiner observed the fractionation problem in university faculties as they experience the centrifugal forces of greater specialization and a tendency to identify more with their distant peers than with their daily working colleagues of other disciplines.[16] For health professionals, joining the professional and special interest associations or subscribing to all the mail-order services created to appeal to secular interests no longer met by family, church, and employer will deplete the resources and energy of even the most gregarious and committed enthusiasts for a profession, a cause, or other special interest. They retreat to their suburban homes for relief and solitude at night, then rush back into the tumult by day. The academic health center could become a better provider for its first public, namely, its students and employees.

The fragmentation problem, contrary to the uprooting and displacement sources of alienation, comes from having *too many* contacts. Having too many specialized memberships and associations can become a source of alienation if each of them is superficial and none of them provides very comprehensively or warmly for human needs. They produce further fragmentation of one's life.

The antidote seems to lie in more comprehensive, closer-to-home organizations and facilities that provide not only services but also more personalized social support or affiliation. Senior centers and teen centers seem to have served this function for these age groups in many communities. Shopping malls have become the surrogate front porch for many teens and elders, bringing the English language another new gerund, "malling." Neighborhood fitness centers have done the same for many young adults, replacing the neighborhood bar for some. Christie Hefner, Hugh Hefner's daughter and now CEO of Playboy Enterprises, thus explained the demise of the fabled Playboy Clubs: "The nightclubs of the sixties and seventies," she said, "have been replaced by the athletic clubs of the eighties."[17]

Parks and recreational centers have served many families with children as places to relate more holistically to the community. For many working adults, the workplace itself has become the primary point of reference for affiliation and an increasing array of services with the growth of employee health promotion programs and facilities, child care services, banking or credit union services, food services, and staff parties. Academic health centers could do the same for children if they were used more creatively for organized after-school activities and linked more effectively with community programs and services. What makes these community facilities and work sites more effective as services is the potential for service providers to know their clients more as whole human beings, not as statistics or categories or fragmented parts of the body or types of problems to be treated. The bureaucratic service provider becomes callous and immunized against feeling too much for the hundreds of clients on her caseload, as a means of self-protection against burnout. But this hardened helper is what makes bureaucratic human services so dehumanizing. This was expressed poetically in the song, "Easy to Be Hard," from the play *Hair: The American Tribal Love-Rock Musical*:

How can people be so heartless?
How can people be so cold?
Especially people who care about strangers,
Who say they care about social injustice.

Do you only care about the bleeding crowd?
How about a needing friend?
I need a friend.

DISEMPOWERMENT VS. COLLECTIVE ACTION

The multiplication of organizations and services at the community
level can be seen as providing resources not only to individuals but
to the community in a more collective sense. They give the community the capacity to pool a wider range of resources and experience
to solve broader social and public health problems. This assumes,
however, that these organizations have a stake in the community
and have some degree of independence or autonomy from their state
or national parent bodies. Unfortunately, much of the proliferation
of organizations has been in the form of branches, affiliates, and
franchises of larger centralized organizations. Such branch operations have limited commitment to the community, their first loyalty
being to the home office. Hence, they sometimes make diffident partners in any community organization effort. They will often contribute to community health events such as health fairs and marathons.
Their motive, however, is more for public relations than for commitment to the community and its development. This distinction does
not bother most organizers of events, and the contributions of such
organizations should not be trivialized. To the community orga-
nizer, however, this distinction becomes more meaningful because
commitment to the community and its development makes a big difference in how the representatives of an organization on a community planning committee behave and contribute.

The academic health center can be an ideal convener for a community coalition to address health services, health protection, or
health promotion issues. It has deep roots in the community, it is not
typically beholden to an out-of-state master, it can cut deals with
local organizations, and it can draw upon vast resources to leverage
commitments and resources from other organizations.

The first task of community organization for academic health centers is to build partnerships and coalitions. Most problems or goals
requiring a community organization effort are by definition larger

than any one organization can be expected to handle, and the stakes in the community issue often affect many different interest groups. For either reason, the solution lies first in getting representation and participation on multi-agency or multi-group committees. Committees can assess and analyze a situation, develop plans, make recommendations to higher levels of government or to specific organizations, but they seldom become implementing or action bodies. A coalition requires clearly specified rules as to the extent to which the academic health center, as convener or sponsor of a community initiative, will be bound by decisions of the group, and how those decisions will be made.

The campus, facilities, personnel, and prestige of the academic health center represent resources to a community far beyond their usual service. Most academic health centers close many of their buildings, some even close their campus after hours, admitting only those who have a medical emergency or a badge. These great edifices could be more extensively used for adult education, self-help groups, fitness programs, health exhibits, and after-school programs for children. The faculty and staff could be more actively engaged and more appropriately rewarded for participation and service in community health affairs beyond their clinical, teaching, and research duties. The University of California School of Public Health at Berkeley noted in its 1986 Accreditation Self-Study:

> A value conflict regarding service is evident in the School, but this has not been confronted on the institutional level. On the one hand, the School encourages faculty service and indeed generates many demands for it. On the other hand, the School does not reward faculty for service involvements. Resulting ambiguities create many pressures for faculty, while the School itself remains unclear about the role of service in fulfilling the School's mission.[18]

Every academic institution I know could say the same. The Institute of Medicine's Committee on the Future of Public Health specifically recommended that "schools of public health should establish firm links with public health agencies so that more faculty have responsibilites in these agencies."[19] For students to become properly trained to take community leadership roles in their health careers, they need community training.[20] Such training will require teaching in the classroom and in the field that is inspired by community experience and community values. Such experience and values should be shared by all disciplines and specialists, not just public health.

Federal public health policy has clearly signaled the intent to turn more of the responsibility for health back to states and communities. Foundations also indicate growing interest in community-level funding for health innovation and development. As described by Alvin R. Tarlov, former president of the Henry J. Kaiser Foundation,

> It stems from a perception among foundations that social change can be effectively fashioned, customized, if you will, through local circumstances by community groups if those groups are empowered to assume responsibility for it. It's a discovery. I don't know where the discovery came from; perhaps California with its direct governance by public referendum has something to do with it. But in the United States there is an accelerating trend to empower local organizations and individuals in an effort to seek change.[21]

CONCLUSION

The evolution of the American community and of academic health centers suggests a convergence of purpose in health but a divergence of values. Communities show signs of reviving their capability and desire to grapple with local health needs and the problems of their populations. Academic health centers, meanwhile, have become increasingly global in their orientation, looking past the problems in their own communities to address the more generalizable health problems of the nation or the world.

Three consequences of the decline of communities in recent decades were alienation, dehumanization of centralized services, and disempowerment of local groups and individuals to cope with the problems of their communities. Recent signs of the revival of community spirit, community-based services, and effective community organization suggest new opportunities for the engagement of academic health centers in community health matters. The future support of community initiatives in health from health professionals will require a generation of students in the health fields receiving more community experience and training. Faculty can offer this only if they, themselves, are actively engaged in community service and research. This will require some revamping of the promotions and tenure criteria.

Finally, academic health centers can make an effective start in support of community health values by putting their own houses in order with programs and benefits for their employees that demonstrate these values to the community. Child care services, employee health promotion programs and facilities, outreach activities for dependents, and more open community use of academic health center facilities all would contribute to a more community-oriented academic environment. Leadership from the academic health center in coordinating community initiatives for health protection and health promotion would put the university more squarely in the fray, but will require sensitivity and generosity in sharing the power and fostering the spirit of self-reliance that has accomplished the revival of communities.

NOTES

Parts of this paper were given as the Alliance Scholar Lecture, the DeHaan Lecture at Emory University, and the Commencement Address at Lowell University. Thanks to Alvin R. Tarlov and my other colleagues at the Henry J. Kaiser Family Foundation for their inspiration and support in developing these thoughts.

1. Larry McMurtry, *The Last Picture Show* (New York: Dial Press, 1966), and *Texasville* (New York: Simon & Schuster, 1987); Garrison Keillor, *Lake Wobegon Days* (New York: Viking, 1985).
2. Peter Collier and David Horowitz, *Destructive Generation: Second Thoughts about the Sixties* (New York: Summit Books, 1989); Todd Gitlin, *The Sixties: Years of Hope, Days of Rage* (New York: Bantam Books, 1988); Max Heirich, *Berkeley 1964: The Spiral of Conflict* (New York: Columbia University Press, 1971); Jonathan Rabinovitz, "People's Park Struggle Resumes after Twenty Years: Berkeley Journal," *New York Times*, April 24, 1989; W. J. Rorabaugh, *Berkeley at War: The 1960s* (New York: Oxford University Press, 1989).
3. John K. Iglehart, "Charting a New Course: A Conversation with Leighton E. Cluff," *Health Affairs* (Spring 1989): 191–202.
4. Alexis de Tocqueville, *Democracy in America* (New York: Macmillan, 1969 [1831]).

5. Marshall McLuhan and Quentin Fiore, *The Medium Is the Massage: An Inventory of Effects* (New York: Bantam Books, 1967).

6. Independent Sector, *Giving and Volunteering in the United States: Findings from a National Survey*, 1988 edition (Washington, D.C.: Independent Sector, 1988).

7. U.S. Bureau of the Census, *Statistical Abstract of the United States: 1989*, 109th edition (Washington, D.C.: U.S. Government Printing Office, 1989).

8. Kenneth Howe, "California's Homeowner Wars: Resident Associations Provide Battleground for Myriad Squabbles," *San Francisco Chronicle*, July 3, 1989. Data from Community Associations Institute and an unpublished University of California at Berkeley study by Stephen Barton and Carol Silverman.

9. Alan B. Durning, *Action at the Grassroots: Fighting Poverty and Environmental Decline* (Washington, D.C.: Worldwatch Institute, 1989).

10. Brian Dumaine, "What the Leaders of Tomorrow See," *Fortune* 120 (July 1989): 48–76.

11. David W. McMillan and David M. Chavis, "Sense of Community: A Definition and Theory," *Journal of Community Psychology* 14(1986): 6–23.

12. Joseph A. Califano, Jr., *America's Health Care Revolution: Who Lives? Who Dies? Who Pays?* (New York: Random House, 1986).

13. David M. Chavis, J. H. Hogge, David W. McMillan, and A. Wandersman, "Sense of Community through Brunswick's Lens: A First Look," *Journal of Community Psychology* 14(1986): 24–40.

14. Pat Schroeder, *Champion of the Great American Family* (New York: Random House, 1989).

15. Eric Foner, *Reconstruction: America's Unfinished Revolution, 1863–1900* (New York: Harper & Row, 1988).

16. Daniel Steiner, "Approaching Ethical Questions: A University Perspective," in this volume.

17. Jon Van Housen, "Let's Get Physical: Vail Valley Athletic Clubs Are Flexing Their Muscles," *Vail Valley* (March 1989).

18. School of Public Health, University of California at Berkeley, *Accreditation Self-Study Report* (Washington, D.C.: Council on Education for Public Health, 1986).

19. Institute of Medicine, *The Future of Public Health* (Washington, D.C.: National Academy Press, 1988).

20. Julie W. Williamson, "Strengthening the Manpower Pool for Community Health Promotion: Opportunities, Obstacles, and Models for Training," consultation paper prepared by the Western Consortium for Public Health (Menlo Park, Calif.: Henry J. Kaiser Family Foundation, 1988).

21. John K. Iglehart, "An Interview with Alvin R. Tarlov," *Health Affairs* (1988).

Conclusion

EDMUND D. PELLEGRINO

VALUES AND ACADEMIC HEALTH CENTERS:

A COMMENTARY AND RECOMMENDATIONS

It is impossible to summarize the variety and richness of these essays. Instead I shall offer some reflections on the thoughts in them, limiting myself to three purposes: to identify the common threads that run through all of the essays, to offer some comments on general ethical aspects of their themes, and to recommend ways in which health-related institutions may expand their concerns about values and translate them into action.

MAJOR THEMES

Individual human beings are identified by the values they espouse and even more so by the values they evidence in their daily decisions and activities. Each of us thus has a physiognomy of values, some configuration of things, beliefs, and ideals for which we are willing to pay, work, fight, suffer, and even, if occasion demands, die. Much of our identity as persons is bound up with these values which we identify as our own and which we continuously sift and rearrange in the course of our lives.

What is true of individuals is also true of collectivities—groups of humans working, living, and deciding together in institutions and communities of all kinds, from the family to the hospital or university. Collectivities, like individuals, also have distinguishing traits; each has a set of values and choices which reveal what it thinks or wants to be communally.

With institutions as with individuals, value choices often, though not always, have moral and ethical implications. A value takes on a moral aspect whenever some quality of good or bad, right or wrong is attached to it in such a way that a duty or obligation is implied. Clearly all values are not moral values. Many of those discussed in these essays are primarily social, economic, cultural, ethnic, or pedagogical. Yet each value can, under certain circumstances, present ethical issues, problems, or dilemmas.

Every author herein started from the proposition that academic health centers and their constituents—hospitals, medical schools, nursing schools, etc.—do indeed have values, that those values influence the behavior of those who work in these institutions and also affect the futures of the students, patients, and communities who depend upon the institutions for certain socially necessary functions.

What seem especially clear are the conflicts of values and the crisis of value identity that characterize academic health centers in our country today. These conflicts arise from the interplay of economic, sociocultural, political, and scientific-technical forces acting upon health centers, both from without and within. The majority of these essays focus on some facet or other of these forces and the value conflicts they generate.

Roger Bulger's opening chapter speaks of the academic health center as a "moral agent," but one in conflict about its essential identity. Five competing models vie today for dominance, each with a primary focus: public interest, social service, university functions, molecular biology, and the status quo. No institution is a pure paradigm of any one model. Each model has traces of the others intermingled with it. But each model entails commitment to a set of values which give the institutions differing ethical priorities. Some of these priorities are in fundamental conflict with the covenant academic health centers have with society to fulfill certain of its specific needs. What the moral mission of academic health centers should be is the central unresolved ethical issue.

Stanley Reiser focuses on the way the values of economic survival may defeat the humane purposes of hospitals and medical schools. Neither economics nor humanitarianism can be sacrificed without mutual damage. At the moment the humane purposes seem particularly endangered by the barriers to care encountered increasingly by poor patients, the excessively long work hours of house staff, the sometimes inadequate supervision of students and house staff by faculty attending physicians, and a series of other manifestations of institutional insensitivity. Fiduciary relationships should, Reiser asserts, be the ethical guideline in teaching and patient care. Reiser suggests that the hospital must become a humane corporation, balancing its fiduciary with its fiscal obligations. Whether such a balance is possible and where the balance should be set are highly problematic.

In a similar vein, Ruth Bulger and Kim Dunn carry the inquiry into the domains of teaching and learning in a dialogue between teacher and student. In eloquent detail they trace the problems of curriculum, teacher-student relationships, and patient care which have been the subject of much criticism for many decades by prestigious commissions, committees, and panels. Despite a spate of recommendations and curricular revisions, some problems remain obdurate: the overloading of the curriculum with scientific and technical detail, the neglect of preventive medicine and public health, faculty rewards for research rather than teaching, the demand on clinical faculties to engage in practice, faculty insensitivity to the needs of patients and students as persons, neglect of family medicine, etc.

Bulger and Dunn emphasize the ethical obligations of medical schools and hospitals, especially the obligations of teachers to address these incongruities. They encourage teachers to conform to the ethical obligation exemplified in the writing of Eric Ashby and the less patriarchal, more person-centered ethical values espoused by Carol Gilligan. Their dialogue underscores the fundamental value conflicts in medical academia and how equally fundamental their remedy must be. They show us too how teaching and learning must be interdigitated.

The university is, like the hospital, a collectivity with values which may sometimes be at variance with those of the society they serve. Daniel Steiner describes the shared desire of universities to maintain autonomy in determining what they teach as well as freedom of the faculty to express opinions that may be contrary to conventional wisdom. By virtue of their stewardship over human knowledge, universities are also called to higher degrees of moral sensitivity than business enterprises.

These values may be threatened in a variety of ways exemplified in the increasingly more frequent liaisons with industry. Here the lure of funding for research may compromise the very viability of the research itself, which cannot thrive without objectivity and freedom in the choice of research problems and communication of results through publication. Industry, on the other hand, emphasizes competitiveness, withholding information to achieve a market advantage. Industry requires emphasis on research topics and results that pay off at the bottom line of profit. Balancing the values of business and those of scholarly inquiry has become a major challenge for today's university.

Universities, Steiner asserts, must resolve these value conflicts internally for a number of reasons: because of their obligation to be morally more responsive than many of society's other institutions; because university faculties in Steiner's opinion are better qualified than others to make judicious decisions on issues relating to academic freedom; and finally, for pragmatic reasons alone, because they must do so or society will intervene via government regulation. It is clear that what universities do is too vital to be left to university faculties who do not exercise their freedoms responsibly.

Robert Coles explores the tensions between institutional and personal values in a very provocative manner through his recollections of two conversations—one with Martin Luther King and one with a medical student. Their words reveal the creative and destructive ways in which individuals may respond to the values of the institutions within which they reside.

King acknowledges the great power of institutions to shape our values and even our characters. But while they are a "big part of the story," they are not the whole story. As King's own life so well attests, institutional values can be changed. It is precisely because of their great power that King set out to change America's values about race relations. The medical student, on the other hand, submits totally to the values of his medical school. "The people who run this place run me," he says. He identifies his whole being, not as a person, but as a medical student. Pretentiously he likens himself to the peasant who, after centuries of oppression, finally speaks out. Unlike the peasant he seeks expiation in psychotherapy.

King's responses are those of a morally mature person who has chosen certain values consciously. They identify him so clearly that they cannot be submerged by unjust institutions. King might blame society for its distorted values but he does not take their power as an excuse for acquiescence. He wants our institutions to have the right values and is courageous enough to speak out for them. The medical student, on the other hand, lacks identity. He has not assimilated his ideals. He is morally malleable because he does not know which values can be compromised and which cannot. He is a prime example of the negative effect of an institution's values on the character of its inhabitants.

It is well to keep in mind both images Coles puts before us. Institutions have an obligation to choose the right kind of values, to shape the right kind of character in those who function within them, and to allow for the expression of personal values. Institutions and their leaders cannot escape responsibility for the ways in which they shape character. Individuals, on the other hand, are morally accountable. They must participate in the establishment of institutional values and oppose them when they are in error. They cannot excuse their own moral failings by blaming their medical schools or teachers. Moral judgment is a responsibility no educated human can evade.

These five essays describe, in a general way, the conflicts and moral dilemmas now besetting academic health centers, universities, and medical schools and the way they impinge upon those who work within these institutions and are served by them. Three authors take these considerations further by illustrating through case histories how value conflicts are successfully and unsuccessfully resolved.

Donald Fredrickson, speaking as a scientist and former director of the National Institutes of Health, traces the history of that institution's response to the ethical challenges in clinical investigation and fetal research. He takes as given that the values of the NIH are the values of science in general, for example, the open and objective presentation of data, respect for the priority of contributions, informed consent, peer review, and institutional review boards to oversee ethical issues in extramural research. The central dilemma is how to preserve the scientific values which are essential to medical progress without violating ethical norms.

When such crucial ethical issues as human experimentation and fetal research arose, the NIH depended upon full and open discussion of the issues, a complete record of every aspect of those discussions, the guidance of committees and panels of experts, and, whenever possible, the promulgation of guidelines rather than rules. Fredrickson believes that the most prudent course for the NIH is to rely on experts to provide the answers. He uses the famed Asilomar conference to illustrate the kind of ethical responsiveness that should motivate scientific investigation. In that instance, the molecular geneticists themselves called for a moratorium on recombinant DNA research until its potential hazards were more fully known.

An even more detailed case history is that of the Beth Israel Hospital in Boston. Mitchell Rabkin, the chief executive of Beth Israel, focuses his essay on the juxtaposition of the special values of a university-affiliated teaching and research hospital with those of the community it serves. Rabkin worked with a clearly established tradition of combining service with teaching and research. The board of trustees set the goal of balancing these diverse responsibilities as a primary element in the hospital's mission.

This is a case history in institutional and administrative style, one which consists of constant awareness of the needs of patients, reenforcement of good patient care by teaching and research, and the importance of developing a knowledge of and dedication to these goals in every member of the hospital community. To this end Rabkin uses the principles of participatory management which keeps workers informed about the mission of the hospital. His focus is on the process of achieving a goal which approximates the ideals of the institution.

What is manifest in the Beth Israel case study is equally manifest in the case of Cook County Hospital described by James Haughton. The key element is the personal example and interest shown by each chief executive officer. Haughton's personal involvement in such details as housekeeping, fresh paint, and the dress and deportment of the house staff manifestly had much to do with raising staff morale and putting the humane purpose of the Cook County Hospital into focus as the ordering value. Like Rabkin, Haughton gives us an example of the indispensible role the CEO plays in establishing the moral tone and the values of the institution.

In a general way Lawrence Green's essay has a normative tone. He inquires into the responsibilities of academic health centers to their contiguous communities. Green examines the societal transformations in community, families, and the professions that characterize recent history. He concludes that academic health centers have an obligation to reverse some of the deleterious social trends he describes. He proposes that the resources of academic health centers be made more available to their immediate communities. Buildings, personnel, and expertise of these centers can be much more imaginatively used to improve the societal conditions of their immediate communities which are often poor, populated by minorities, economically depressed, and rife with social ills. Green's paper calls for a specific kind of commitment few academic health centers have made or are currently willing to make.

Each of these authors makes the strong recommendation that value conflicts within academic health centers and between these centers and the communities in which they reside be settled by open dialogue and discussion. The goal of dialogue is clarification of the nature, source, and strength of the conflicts, out of which consensus on values will emerge. H. Tristram Engelhardt's paper provides the historical background and defines the philosophical necessity for this mode of decision making in democratic pluralistic societies.

Engelhardt reviews the history of morality in the western world leading to our present stage of moral pluralism and secular humanism. Since the Middle Ages there has been a progressive loss of belief in a universally applicable, objective order of morality. There is no longer a commonly accepted idea of human nature on which moral consensus might be based. In a secular humanist society there is no common set of values, no way to rank values against each other, and thus no common grounding for a moral life. Instead, public institutions must turn to the peaceful resolution of controversy by consensus among those affected by decisions. The only limitations are truth, respect for persons, and tolerance. In this way a society or institution chooses for itself what values it shall accept and reject.

Thus there is no canonical set of values automatically acceptable to all the members of secular pluralist societies. Such a canon is possible only in private institutions whose members come together precisely because they do share a common ideology, a religion, or some other source of values. But in public institutions, Engelhardt argues, values must be chosen by common consent and may thus vary from time to time and place to place.

Stephen Toulmin steps back and asks for a long look at the idea of institutional ethics, what the hospital has in fact become in today's world, and the way the idea of institutional ethics is construed.

What he sees is a dark story. The hospital has been transformed by economic, bureaucratic, legal, and technological forces into a tyrannical organization which limits professional discretion and ethics in the name of institutional procedure. He speaks of the Creonization of the hospital, metaphorically likening it to Creon's tyrannical imposition of his will on Antigone by forbidding her to provide suitable burial for her brother.

Toulmin feels hospitals can no longer fully recover their innocence but must instead work within the constraints institutions place on ethics. This means that we must seek to modify and minimize the inevitable distortions of ethics that occur in today's institutions. We must seek out whatever possibilities for moral good still remain and optimize them. While the story is therefore dark, there is some small light left if we have a will to seek it out.

SOME ETHICAL REFLECTIONS

Ethical reflection may take four forms: descriptive, in which the moral values actually exhibited are detailed; analytical, in which the concepts themselves are clarified or critically examined as to meaning; normative, in which the values that ought to be exhibited are formally argued for; and foundational, in which the underlying presuppositions and concepts are examined and defended. A complete moral philosophy of academic health centers would include all four dimensions.

Most of the essays in this collection are descriptive in nature. They concentrate on the values and conflicts between values actually exhibited in today's health centers. Engelhardt and Toulmin are more analytical, providing a critical inquiry into the general concept of moral values and the processes of choosing among them. Toulmin examines the nature of health sciences centers as agents of institutional ethics. This is a foundational issue, as is the question of what defines a "good" as opposed to a "bad" center.

For the most part, normative statements expressing explicit arguments for the primacy of certain values over others, except as prima facie assertions, are eschewed. Yet most of the authors at least implicitly assume that some values are better than others and that conflicts should be resolved in one way rather than another. Assumptions of this kind, for example, underlie Ruth Bulger's assertion of the ethics of teaching, Green's delineation of the social and community responsibility of academic centers, and Fredrickson's starting point in the ethics of good science.

Without negating the evident value of dialogue and consent, I maintain that these are means to moral conclusions and not ends. The moral validity of the values that should characterize an academic health center must still be sought. Procedure, no matter how appealing, cannot by itself establish what is a good health center. Here organizations and communities—even within the constraints on consensus imposed by Engelhardt—can argue for or accept morally dubious or morally wrong values. For example, Engelhardt himself has proposed a set of values and virtues for medicine derived from the need to accommodate the values of the competitive market place. Many would agree and many may disagree. How is the dispute, even in democratic pluralist societies, to be resolved? Would a majority vote give moral legitimacy to dumping the poor patient or skimming off the paying patient or putting the interests of the physician ahead of beneficence?[1]

In our pluralist society there will be staunch defenders of each of the five models set out by Roger Bulger. Manifestly these models cannot all be pursued with the same vigor or simultaneously. Is there something built into the very concept of an academic health center that renders some values morally untenable and others morally desirable? Certainly in the successful case histories (NIH, Beth Israel, and Cook County), certain values were taken as the normative guidelines for decision making. Could hospitals or academic health centers that rejected these values be able to function in morally defensible ways? Are not some values and obligations of necessity built into the very idea of an academic health center? Does not such a center enter into an implicit covenant with society to behave in certain ways not subject to endless variation or debate?

This problem becomes more acute when we ponder Toulmin's disturbing picture of the hospital as a tyrant which displaces professional and personal ethics. What are the obligations of professionals who in good conscience cannot accept the values of the organization because they violate other values, such as the good of patients? Even if the wrong institutional values were arrived at by consensus they would have to be resisted. There is a higher good than consensus, and there is a consequent moral obligation on certain occasions to resist and to disobey the dominant value system. History abounds in examples of whole societies and organizations that have zealously adopted immoral values. Institutions, like humans, are susceptible to moral pathologies, but without knowing what values are normative we cannot judge or reject moral pathology.

One can agree with Engelhardt's analysis of the historical erosion of common moral values but one need not agree that the effort to ground the moral life in some set of commonly held human values is hopeless. If the light Toulmin sees at the end of the tunnel is to be reached, we need a more critical examination of what academic health centers are, what they should be, who we are as health professionals, and who and what we should be. We need a closer definition of the values, moral and otherwise, that we should exhibit in our institutions and in our personal behavior as physicians, nurses, administrators, teachers of medicine, and students.

In short, the normative and foundational aspects of values and ethics in the academic health centers need to be reexamined in a fresh dialogue as Engelhardt urges, but also in dialectic—in a critical appraisal of the concept, the phenomenology, and the ethics of collective human actions. We need a moral philosophy on which to base our moral assertions, one which will seek consent but will not rest on consent alone. A moral philosophy is more than ethics as it is conceived today, it is an inquiry into the reasons why we should be ethical, why we should act in certain ways, and why some things should never be done.

The moral philosophy of institutions is a subject still in its early stages of development. What does it mean to say that an academic health center is a moral agent? Can a collectivity be a moral agent? How is responsibility distributed in a collectivity? Is there some final authority who can be blamed or praised for the results? What about the ethics of cooperation? When does one become an accomplice in unethical behavior? How close can one come to morally dubious actions and still be innocent of wrongdoing? What are the criteria for justifiable moral disobedience?

Finally, the quest for some ordering of moral principles must not be abandoned. There is a need for values that become the standard against which to measure the ethical performance of institutions. Without such a standard we cannot put conflicting values into a hierarchical relationship. Some might propose the primacy of the physician-patient relationship. I would phrase this somewhat differently as the healing relationship—the covenant of trust between the vulnerable, exploitable, dependent, fearful sick and those who voluntarily offer to heal and help them, either as individual practitioners or as functioning members of a health care institution.[2]

Yes, the values of good science must be observed. Yes, the values of efficient management and economic operation have a place. Yes, the canons of good teaching and learning must be respected. Yes, the principle of communal dialogue is valid. The intermingling of these values in the modern academic health center is inescapable. In the medical school it is true that research, teaching, and learning have primacy; in the hospital patient care has primacy. But wherever these values are in open conflict the needs of the sick must be given extra weight, for it is on their behalf that the whole enterprise exists in the first place.

SOME RECOMMENDATIONS

These essays provide a rich commentary on an important problem: the intersection of moral values integral to the character and work of academic health centers. With genuine diffidence but responsive to the task assigned me, I would make the following recommendation: that the dialogue, discussion, and dialectic be continued. This could be done in a variety of ways, four of which I propose in conclusion.

A task force could be convened to examine what values should characterize a good academic health science center. This task force should be asked to draft a statement of commitments or a code of common values to guide member organizations and to assure the public that these organizations understand their moral obligations.

CEOs must be encouraged to conduct periodic inventories of the values actually being exhibited in their institutions, to determine whether they are consistent with the mission of the institution and with the guidelines of what values should predominate. Clinical pathological conferences are now increasingly the practice in clinical bioethics. Administrative ethical postmortems can be used with equal effectiveness to examine the moral probity of institutional decisions.

Health care institutions should accept the responsibility for teaching all constituencies—faculty, staff, students, boards of trustees—the essentials of ethical decision making and ethical discourse. The day is past when moral judgment could be made without some knowledge of the way ethical issues are identified and conflicts resolved. Far more important than formal teaching, however, is the responsibility for practicing those moral values which are consistent with the obligations we assume when we undertake to care for the sick, to teach, to learn, and to add to human knowledge through research.

We should encourage the establishment of a corps of teachers and researchers in ethics in each health science center. Professionally trained ethicists and health professionals knowledgeable in ethics exist now in many medical and nursing schools, but they have yet to receive the unqualified support of the CEOs. The CEOs themselves should raise value and ethical questions as they confront the institution and thus exert moral as well as managerial leadership in a time of confusion and doubt. An opportunity exists to restore moral integrity to the health care enterprise. I hope it will not be lost.

NOTES

These comments were made in situ, so to speak, without prior access to any of the manuscripts.

1. H. T. Engelhardt, Jr., and M. A. Rie, "Morality for the Medical-Industrial Complex: A Code of Ethics for the Mass Marketing of Health Care," *New England Journal of Medicine* 319 (October 1988): 1086–1089.
2. Edmund D. Pellegrino, "The Healing Relationship: The Architectonics of Clinical Medicine," in *The Clinical Encounter: The Moral Fabric of the Patient-Physician Relationship, Philosophy and Medicine*, vol. 4, ed. Earl Shelp (Dordrecht: D. Reidel Publishing Co., 1983), pp. 153–172.

NOTES ON CONTRIBUTORS

ROGER J. BULGER, M.D., president, Association of Academic Health Centers, Washington, D.C., has held a wide variety of administrative positions in health professional education. In his writings he weaves together concern for the humanistic, policy, and scientific dimensions of health care to portray the unique place of this enterprise in society.

RUTH ELLEN BULGER, Ph.D., director of the Division of Health Sciences Policy, Institute of Medicine, National Academy of Sciences, Washington, D.C., has had a career as a medical scientist and is now a policy analyst. She focuses on the nature of education in her thinking and writing.

ROBERT COLES, M.D., professor of psychiatry and medical humanities, Harvard University, is a psychiatrist, educator, and author who has explored the moral, political, and spiritual life of children.

KIM DUNN is an M.D./Ph.D. student, University of Texas Health Science Center at Houston, and past chair, Organization of Student Representatives, Association of American Medical Colleges. She combines interests in education, social action, patient care, and public health as one of the national student leaders in health care.

H. TRISTRAM ENGELHARDT, JR., Ph.D., M.D., professor of medicine and community medicine, Baylor College of Medicine, is a powerful speaker and writer with a keen interest in Texas traditions. He brings together an understanding of philosophical, medical, and historical forces to illuminate significant issues in health care.

DONALD S. FREDRICKSON, M.D., Washington, D.C., is an eminent scientist who has directed the National Institutes of Health and other major institutions for the doing of science and science policy and has written about scientific processes and meaning.

LAWRENCE W. GREEN, Dr. P.H., vice-president for health promotion, Henry J. Kaiser Family Foundation, Menlo Park, California, has been a national leader in the fields of health promotion and disease prevention, making a strong case for the need for community involvement in the nation's health care.

JAMES G. HAUGHTON, M.D., M.P.H., medical director, King/Drew Medical Center, Los Angeles, has been a leader in introducing change into the hospital and public health systems that he has overseen in his long and illustrious career in public service.

EDMUND D. PELLEGRINO, M.D., professor of medicine and director, Institute for the Advanced Study of Ethics at Georgetown University, Washington, D.C., has held a variety of administrative positions in health care and education and has made numerous intellectual contributions to the study of relationships among medicine, philosophy, and ethics.

MITCHELL T. RABKIN, M.D., president, Beth Israel Hospital, Boston, Massachusetts, and professor of medicine, Harvard Medical School, is a distinguished physician and hospital director known for his innovative administrative performance. He has been a pioneer in introducing ethical and nursing reforms into hospitals.

STANLEY JOEL REISER, M.D., Ph.D., Griff T. Ross Professor of Humanities and Technology in Health Care, University of Texas Health Science Center at Houston, is a physician, historian, ethicist, and educator whose interests in technology development and human values have brought him international prominence.

DANIEL STEINER, LL.B., vice-president and general counsel, Harvard University, has worked for over two decades on a wide variety of problems related to institutional values and the ethical aspects of a university's activities.

STEPHEN TOULMIN, Ph.D., Avalon Foundation Professor in Humanities, Department of Philosophy, Northwestern University, has far-reaching interests which range from cosmology to casuistry and from epistemology to clinical ethics. The consummate scholar, he portrays with depth some of the basic philosophical issues of human history.